THE FIRST EDITION OF

AN ENGLISH YEAR

CONSISTS OF

TWO THOUSAND AND FIFTY

NUMBERED COPIES OF WHICH

NINETEEN HUNDRED AND FIFTY

ARE FOR SALE

This is number

803

AN
ENGLISH
YEAR

AN
ENGLISH
YEAR

NAN
FAIRBROTHER

NEW YORK
ALFRED A. KNOPF
MCMLIV

THIS IS A
BORZOI BOOK

PUBLISHED BY
ALFRED A. KNOPF, INC.

FIRST AMERICAN EDITION

Published in Great Britain by Chatto & Windus
under the title of CHILDREN IN THE HOUSE

CONTENTS

PART ONE

WINTER

THERE ARE ALL SORTS OF REASONS WHY this week after Christmas is a specially low ebb in the year. Not anti-climax, for one had not, at this grown-up age, looked forward to anything in this season of merry-making by appointment. Only dismally and confidently to the extra work. So that we are tired, and the children crotchety from too many pleasures, the house is messy with paper decorations, and Spring such a very long way off.

That is really the trouble. Since Christmas is in the darkest days of the year, we always feel it must be the depth of winter too, when really it is only the beginning, with the last leaves scarcely fallen from the elms by the stream. "As the light grows longer, the cold grows stronger." The Farmer across the orchard says it every year, but still each Boxing Day I go out into the garden and look confidently for Spring bulbs to be showing, determined shoots of daffodils, and hyacinth buds packed as tight as pomegranate seeds. And every year I am disappointed at the uncompromising Winter.

But there is still a minor pleasure this last week of the year. Ask anyone at all whether they have enjoyed Christmas, and the answer is unfailingly the same.

"Did you have a good Christmas?"

"Yes, thank you. Quiet, you know, but very nice."

I ask everyone I meet on the farm or in the village, and count how many times they answer just exactly that. And always the "Quiet, you know" comes in a tone of mild surprise, as if they had expected something quite different—drums and cymbals all day long, and shouting from the roof-tops.

Not that they were quiet at all really, with the whole family together, half a dozen excited children, and carols and the wireless. But still the domestic uproar is nothing beside some cloudy unconscious idea in the background of their minds of what Christmas *might* be like in the way of noise. Choirs of rejoicing angels perhaps, and "everyone suddenly burst out singing." So that each year they are vaguely astonished that after all it has been only the ordinary noise they made themselves.

Still I never feel that Christmas is quiet, especially not today when we have had our yearly party for John and Peter, who are three and four. They are always just the same, our parties, and their unfailing success is quite simple—we live in an old farmhouse with two staircases. One is wide with a banister, the other low and secret and painted bright blue; the Blue Stairs, the children call it, and play at shops with the steps for shelves.

The only other things that matter are an enormous farmhouse tea for the mothers and nannies, and a pleasant imperturbable Comforter for when children cry. For the party is very simple and always the same. The children arrive with brushed hair and best clothes, their attendant mothers hovering over them to watch and smile. They play quietly with the Christmas toys put out for them, each in separate corners of the nursery until tea-time, engrossed in their own game, ignoring each other as small children do, even at parties. At tea they sit round the table like angels, shyly exercising their best party manners and eating almost nothing. For children of three and four, it seems, however sturdy, always eat nothing, and in any case the tea is not meant for them.

After that the real party begins. The mothers and nannies, reassured by so much good behaviour, forget their charges and settle down to endless cups of tea and local gossip. And the rest is simple. Without a word of suggestion, the children rush to the other end of the house, arrange themselves in a line, and circle in an endless screaming crocodile up the big staircase, round the landings, down the Blue Stairs, and across the hall. No one organizes it, it simply happens. And it never palls. Conjurers, films, Punch and Judy, all may lose their magic for children too small to sit still, but never this.

Up—round—down—across. Up—round—down—across. I wonder if they say it to themselves like learning to knit. From time to time, with no warning, like a flock of starlings, they suddenly all turn round at once and go down the up staircase and up the other. Nothing else.

The Comforter must shut herself in the nursery, for the din is appalling to any mere grown-up, and she need only bob out from time to time to pick up any casualties who sit and wail. Luckily children as small as this seem to bounce like rubber balls, and even a fall from top to bottom of the staircase is soon forgotten in a dip in the bran-tub and the impatience to be back again.

So children roused from sleep in the night settle back

impatiently, not to oblivion, but to some other world more real and vivid than our shadowy darkness. As if we had brought them out from a party and they listened, not to what we were saying, but still to the noise going on without them beyond the door.

This stair game lasts for an hour, sometimes more, for their staying power is fantastic. I can only wonder what goes on in the minds of such strange and alien beings. Round and round they go, with the drugged concentration of some savage rite, keeping always equidistant, ignoring their friend who falls by the way, seeing only the blue silk party socks and the climbing legs of the one in front.

As soon as the mothers appear, they slacken and stop, turning back to ordinary children. Perhaps they stop from exhaustion, but perhaps because they know that so intoxicating a game would surely be forbidden. For children are cunning enough behind their innocent faces, though prudent might be a kinder word to describe them.

Then there are coats to sort out, gloves and boots and scarves, all the ritual of wrapping up small creatures against the Winter. And off they go into the swallowing dark of the orchard, leaving me to remember that one of the compensations of children's parties is that when I have bundled my own two off to bed and helped the Comforter to clear up the tea things, there is still the evening left to recover in, and to read my book in quiet.

PETER: "I like parties. There are lots of people and they all talk at once. You can stop in the door, and you can't hear what they say, but it sounds like rooks cawing, and I like it."

So I told him about pushing your fingers in and out of

your ears when a noise is going on, so that it sounds like ducks quacking. But I did not tell him that I used to do it to pass the time in school prayers, nor, worse still, that until I was really quite old I thought that "Hallowéd be Thy name" was "Hello be Thy name," and that it sounded quite reasonable, like the telephone.

I suppose everyone's mind has odd patches of ignorance which somehow survive long after they should, as a chance patch of snow may stay untrodden, even in a busy street.

THE red-wings have arrived on the farm, late this year, for they generally come over Christmas, but perhaps I only have not seen them till now, busy in the house. They are very tame (though John does not think so), flying along the hedges just in front of us with their wavy flight and chirrupy song. They let us come so close that we can see their walrus moustaches and George Robey eyebrows, and when they fly, the rust-brown patch on the side of their bodies which gives them their inaccurate exotic name. They are very much birds of the trees here, not like the fieldfares, which seem to be always on the ground, though I have not seen the fieldfares yet this Winter. But the long-tailed tits are here, in groups of eight to twelve about the orchard, and great flocks of larks with their purring Winter song like sweet sewing-machines.

"SMALL boys," I thought, as Christmas was suddenly near and I must find presents for John and Peter, "boys will play with a dolls'-house just as much as little girls." But I was wrong. For I found them one in a local sale, painted it with roses on the walls, made new furniture from odd bits of wood, and hid it all carefully behind an elaborate barricade of chairs and trunks and dust-sheets till Christmas morning.

They greeted it with delight, and divided it in half as they do always, marking out their separate spheres of influence. For they know very well by now that they can only play together without quarrelling if they each have their own private preserve and respect each other's territory.

Then they set about playing, for they did play, though not at all like little girls. All the furniture was piled into trucks (for removal-vans), pulled round the garden twice, and dumped in pathetic small heaps under the lilacs, chairs and tables with their legs helplessly in the air, and framed cigarette-card pictures of railway-engines.

But luckily it is Winter, and the mouse-trapping season again, and the poor dead mice make wonderful dolls for a dolls'-house. So now John and Peter play all day long at houses, developing their domestic instincts in what I can only hope is a most promising way, since they really must learn one day to help me wash the dishes. For mice are the exact size for the dolls' furniture, and look endearingly snug in a yellow-painted cot tucked in with a blue and white checked counterpane. They are always beautifully arranged, their whiskers uncrushed, their tail curled round as elegantly as a sleeping cat's, their delicate silky paws lying on the cover like a Victorian invalid's.

All the same, they have their drawbacks as dolls. To begin with, dead mice are incurably languid. They will not stand at the cooking-stove, nor wash up at the sink, nor even sit at table, except like the Mad Hatter's Dormouse. All the games have to be sleeping games, or bathing and putting to bed. Then they have fleas, though the children seem not to mind. "They don't bite," they say, "they don't like the taste of people. They go away to find another mouse to eat."

The mice themselves do not last long, of course. An hour or two of *rigor mortis* and a day as dolls, two days if the weather is very cold, though much less if they are wrapped in a handkerchief for shawl and taken to real bed in loving earnest. The children seem not to notice the gathering smell, but I pick them up by the tail, rather squeamishly by this time, and fling them over the hedge. For there are always plenty more for the catching, though it does seem a sad Massacre of the Innocents. House-mice I would not mind killing, for they are furtive and smelly animals, but these wood-mice which come in from the garden in cold weather are exquisite little creatures. Still, I remember that on an average there are four mouse skulls in every pellet sent up by our pair of barn-owls, and it does not seem to matter very much how they die. At least I set my traps so finely that the victims know nothing of dying except the taste of butter, so sudden the trap is and so decisive. Butter, for they scorn our ration cheese, and will eat only butter or milk chocolate. I once caught seven in succession with the same piece of butter, the record for the house, but it means setting the trap so finely that one's nerves too become unbearably taut, and the trap going off unexpectedly is as shattering as a sudden explosion. Getting up on Winter mornings, there are two interests. Have the pipes frozen? Are there any mice in the traps? I try out the pipes, and the children go to look for mice.

I am only afraid that I may catch my tame mouse by mistake, though tame is not the right word; indifferent would be nearer. For after a day of taming children single-handed, since their father is away at the wars, I find I have very little enthusiasm left for taming mice in the evenings. But I go about my business, and the mouse goes about his, though he does nothing that I can make out in this crumbless room except run round and round the skirting-board in sudden swift rushes followed by complete immobility, when only his eyes move, as if in terror. All the small birds and animals move like this, in nervous jerks between tense stillness, and watching them we become aware of a life of constant fear, controlled only by hunger and cold and the urge to reproduce.

He comes in, my companion, through a hole in the cupboard of my sitting-room, but I wish he would leave my things alone. Before Christmas I had a bag of hazel-nuts there, for the toes of Christmas stockings, but they all disappeared. How he made off with them I cannot imagine, unless he brought a friend and they carried them away like the old story of the rats with the egg, a story which everyone tells, but no one has ever seen happen at first hand. In any case, he seems not to be able to crack his Christmas nuts, for ever since we have heard them bouncing about behind the skirting-boards, upstairs and down, rattling all over the house like a box of marbles.

And to this rattling accompaniment, and with the yellow jasmine outside the window tapping and scratching on the glass because it is a windy night, I sit and try to like Matisse. For I was given at Christmas a book of reproductions of his paintings, and I have tried ever since to like his colours. For that, they tell me, is what I must like. But it is no good. Perhaps he is simply one of the many blind spots I was born with, and in the end he will be with all the other possible pleasures I have lost for ever, like reading Greek, or living in a desert, or liking red wine. It is sad, a deprivation, a narrowing of one's life.

Some painters (or writers or composers) one can look at and not like. One sees what they are doing, one can judge, but either they do not seem good enough, or for us they are unsympathetic. But with Matisse, quite simply I cannot see what he is doing.

Here he is, orange, pink, and jade green, and try as I will I cannot make them compose. The orange is a warm earthy colour, the pink as melting as Renoir's, and the green a sharp acid like turquoise blue and Chinese yellow. They belong to too different ranges, make a discord I have not yet learnt to like.

His many patterns worry me too: a dress, a wallpaper, and the design of the picture, all at once. It is as if he sang too many tunes together, like some of Bach's music which is too difficult for me to sort out the different melodies and I hear only a lovely jumble. But for me Matisse's jumble is not lovely, only distracting. Perhaps I shall never like him, but still I shall try again one day, for all kinds of doors open of themselves as one grows older and more various.

And Matisse perhaps we must enjoy for the sensuous delight in the colours themselves, as even in music which we do not like for its content we can still enjoy the actual sound the instruments are making. But there are other pleasures in colour than direct delight in the colour itself, pleasures which the English appreciate more easily. For the immediate delight of the senses is a gift which northerners do not keep through their adolescence, but must recover again as they grow adult. There are colours which imply what we expect, like a syncopated rhythm, or the variations of a poetic metre. So that we have in our mind at the same time both the colour in front of us and the colour we expected. There is a keen intellectual satisfaction in the under-statement of Mabuse's greyish faces, the over-emphasis of Monet's blue shadows. And if we first saw Botticelli's *Birth of Venus* in black and white, we could never guess the colours. A naked figure floating over a calm sea in a shower of roses, warm, sunny, and delicious. But not at all. The light, says Pater, is "mere sunless dawn," the sky and sea cold grey, the wan pink roses "embrowned a little." And because we know that roses are fresh and pink, and fine Mediterranean weather an unlikely postcard blue, Botticelli's colours are part of the haunting sadness we remember of him. Braque's dark mud colours, Dérain's greenish-greys, have the same fascination, they imply the colours we expect like a rhythm off the beat.

But first we must know the basic rhythm they all work on, not only for colour, but for form. Before we look at pictures we have already looked at the world and seen it, for so we imagine, as it really is. Certainly what we see is for each of us the only authentic reality. How nearly our own vision corresponds to our next-door neighbour's we can only know if we learn to paint. "The snow is white," I say, "with blue shadows." "No," says my companion, "the snow is palest pink and the shadows are brownish." If we could put it down in paint we might find that the world we each of us see exists for no one but ourself, though much more likely it would be only a hackneyed reproduction of the common vision. For surely there are two things which make a painter: a different vision of reality, and the technical power to communicate it. If he is to be a good painter, the artist must also be able to communicate it with beauty, that difficult word which includes tortured Christs as well as radiant Madonnas.

However ordinary our own conception of the world, it serves us as the accepted theme of which every painter's vision is a variation. And without the known theme to correlate them, how could the variations enrich each other? How could we reconcile Canaletto and Van Gogh? El Greco and Boucher?

Some painters, like Bellini and Raoul Dufy, are for us English essentially foreign. We share neither the ardent devotion of the one, nor the sophisticated gaiety of the other. To see the world as they do is to realize, for a moment of sympathy, new and unexpected ways of living.

For each of us there must be a painter to whose vision our own most nearly corresponds. For many English I think it would be Constable, so that we like him first, not for *how* he sees, but for *what* he sees: the English country and climate. For no one like Constable so paints our mercurial English weather.

BUT the English weather now is not mercurial, it is a dead frigidity, and how I hate this ungenerous starveling Winter with its monotony of cold.

> *Custom lies upon thee with a weight*
> *Heavy as frost,*

said Wordsworth, and so it is a weight, this shuddering cold, a burden of numb death. And mean. Mean and shut in. Muffled clothes and shut doors and careful gestures to keep in the hoarded warmth. Even the snow is niggardly, a dusting of dry salt between stiff grasses crystallized with frost, like angelica for Christmas cakes. And on the dry roads the faint powder of snow follows in dirty flurries behind the car-wheels, like dust in the Summer so very long ago.

Here we live as close to the seasons as the Middle Ages did, sighing through the Winter, longing for the Spring. "Wynter wakeneth al my care," said a fourteenth-century poet, and so it does mine, waiting through the dark months to "Welcom somer, with thy sonne softe." But in this dead landscape it is an effort of imagination even to remember the "summer season when soft was the sun." Now only the smoke from the trains is warm and free and alive, billowing in white clouds, melting like ghosts through the spikey trees.

Beyond a certain degree of cold, one ceases to be pitiful and becomes savage. I am no longer sorry for the unhappy fluffed-up birds searching for food, or the miserable frost-blackened evergreens in the garden. I would like the winds to grow colder and colder until all life is destroyed. I would like the flesh peeled off my bones, and the trees killed to the ground. When living things become as wretched as this, all life seems only an invading fungus which the earth suffers with disgust. I would like the rocks swept clean and bare again, the sea rid of its slimey life, and the whole world immaculate with the invulnerable perfection of polar ice.

But Peter sat with rapt unseeing eyes and said slowly: "Tomorrow. If it's fine. If it's a fine day. Tomorrow if it's a fine day," like Alfred Prufrock. Then a long pause. "If it's a fine day tomorrow we can go for a picnic."

Dear Peter. For a week the frost has not melted on the grass even at midday. "But if I knew," I thought, "what special thing he remembers as magic from last Summer's picnics a lifetime ago, we might be able to do it by the nursery fire in comfort." And now today, since it is not actually snowing, Peter thinks we might set off. But at last I have found the special thing which makes his picnic. It is lemonade.

ME: "Where do you want to go for your picnic?"
PETER: "Anywhere. It doesn't matter. Just a picnic."
ME: "What do you want to do?"
PETER: "Nothing. Just have a picnic."

WINTER

ME: "What sort of a picnic?"

PETER: "A picnic with lemonade."

At last. But perhaps even now it is not easy, for children tell us so cryptically little. Everyone knows that picnic lemonade must be fizzy, and drunk chocking from the bottle, but perhaps it must also be sitting on the grass with your head tipped back to drink, and your eyes shut red against the sun, with the fields and trees blue by contrast when you open them again.

Looking back, the moments of intense pleasure which have lasted from childhood were always as complicated and unpredictable as that. But Peter thinks it all comes out of the bottle with the lemonade. For me it had to be a bottle with a glass marble stopper, which you forced in with a pop. And then there was always the tantalizing decision, whether to break the bottle and keep the marble, or to take it all back to the shop, where the man would give you a penny which would buy two marbles. It seems sad to have to decide so early between prudence and pleasure.

So today, since it is not snowing, and since the cold is more manageable now the wind has dropped, we have been for Peter's picnic. Not indeed with lemonade, but with chocolate biscuits from a Christmas parcel, which he says will do instead. We went to the woods, since they are sheltered, to pick the box and yew which grow wild on the chalk hills, and to look for the Irish woodcutters.

In the thin Winter landscape the crowded trees are close and mysterious, making their own world. It is easy to understand how the legends of all countries have peopled the woods with strange creatures. The willing suspension of disbelief is easier when we are shut in, and in this world enclosed from outside reality anything might happen without surprise. Perhaps it is because illusion is more vivid in a confined space that Proust's re-created lost world is so intensely real, since, for all the pink may and the moons like oranges, he is an indoor writer. Balbec is most vividly evoked as a view from the dining-room window, the sea is a reflection on the furniture of his bedroom, the whole sweep of the coast is only a theatre backcloth for Albertine's boyish charms.

The woods were very quiet, not simply without sound, but, as always in woods on windless Winter days, a deliberate listening stillness. At first the children sang and shouted to destroy the silence, as one runs wildly across untrodden snow, but soon they walked quietly on the thick leaves, listening for the smallest sound like nervous animals.

Then we found the woodcutters with their great red tractor dragging chains, and their cheerful fire. The children threw on sticks and laughed to hear them crackle and see the sparks fly up like fireworks, and we all said what a pity that we had no chestnuts to roast. And with a wink at me which would have been a nudge in the ribs if I had stood close enough, the woodcutters told the children tall stories about Ireland. So tall indeed that even the children were suspicious. "Is it true?" they asked all the way home. "Is it true, Dardy? Is it true?"

Poor little things, they need so badly to *know*. "No, Dardy. Did he really do it? Dar*dee*. Tell me. Is it true? Dardy. *Dardy*." Such a pathetic cry for help in their struggle to make for themselves a stable and coherent world from the disconnected chaos which surrounds them. But still it seems unkind to call the merry wood-cutter a liar, and children have no half-measures.

Peter, who is a thoughtful child, wants everything clear right from the beginning. "Where did it all come from? All this? Who made it all?" And since his serious mind digests so carefully everything he is given, it seems unforgivable laziness to put him off with nonsense. So I took a deep breath and tried to make a version of Darwin for the Very Young. How serious and absurd parents must look from the outside.

But the Evolution of Species will not go into words of one syllable, and I cannot think Darwin would even guess what it was that I overheard Peter trying to explain to John.

"Well." Even Peter seemed to feel that it needed a deep breath. "Well. First there was only water. Then there were bits of jelly. Then these growed into fishes. Then the fishes got better and better and they growed into animals." (You can almost see the arms and legs sprouting in his mind, like a fern-frond unrolling in a nature film.) "And the animals got better and better and they growed into people." (It all took about ten years at the most, one feels.) "And the people get better and better" (this is his own addition), "and when I get married she'll be nicer than Dardy."

It must all be very comforting for him, though John is not really interested. "But it isn't any good to ask them where the bits of jelly came from," Peter goes on with great scorn, "because they don't know." It is disheartening rather to have man's million-year ignorance exposed by a four-year-old.

But John never would ask. If he thinks of anything at all before he plunges into his pleasant day, it is how to make it even more delightful. For he finds life enormous and continual fun. The dullest routine of meals and bathing and going to bed, he turns to hilarious games. Even the passing sorrow he embraces with such generous abandon, standing in the middle of the room, crying at the top of his voice, the tears streaming down in rivers, that his misery seems simply a different sort of pleasure. I need only pull a face at him for his sobs to turn to delighted chuckles.

I should have liked him for a brother, but I think he is not at all what Peter would have chosen. In fact he says not, constantly and intensely. "I *hate* John. I hate him. I'll never talk to him again. Not all my life. *Never*. I wish he would die. Now. This minute. Die dead."

This minute yes, but next minute they are rolling on the rug together like friendly dogs. Playing Bumble Puppy they call it, and never cry however much they tumble about, knowing, no one better, the exact hair's-breadth difference between accident and spite.

WE were wakened this morning by the swans flying over, a beat of feathery wings with a curious little moaning sound between as if their joints creaked. There they went, their necks stretched out against the empty blue sky, dazzling white in the sun while we were still in shadow. They are going to Ireland, I suppose, for they flew due west, to the Gulf Stream of the west coast until their lake here thaws out again. But they always seem to be heading straight for fairy-land, such a curiously emotional effect they have on the watcher, so that we are left swallowing hard and eagerly believing all the legends of magic powers and princes turned to birds.

Well, I hope they find good mud in their Celtic Twilight, or fat worms, or whatever it is their digestive systems turn to such unreasonable beauty.

Because when the swans leave it means their lake is frozen over, we have been today to see. A reservoir it is really, though one would never guess, with water for the canals. But the canals are closed now for the war, and the reservoir overgrown and neglected. And there on the level ice the skaters make a Breughel arabesque in variations of black in the cold reflected light. If one believes in "pure" painting, then I suppose the skaters should make just the same picture if they ran about a flat, frosty field in the same pattern. But it would not do at all. All the magic would be gone. For without realizing, one is conscious always of the brittle, translucent ice, the greenish water beneath, the water-weeds and sleeping fishes. And even for the purist, whose sterile waters grow no nymphs and scarcely even fishes, the life of the picture would drain away through the solid meadow like static electricity. On the lake the figures are balanced by movement on the narrow blades of their skates, precariously supported over yielding depths, their spacing and attitudes linked together in a vital pattern by the tensile strength of the ice. On the field they would only run about aimlessly to keep warm in the cold.

And so indeed did we. For the great objection to skating, and it is quite unanswerable, is that when it is cold enough to freeze the lake, it is too cold for reasonable creatures to rush through the air at the speed of skating.

"Can we come again yesterday?" the children said, always vague about their tenses. "Can we come again every day?" they said, cold but enchanted. "Come and walk on top of the water?"

But no, we can't. It is really too cold. Tomorrow we will go and slide instead on the ice of the moat in the humps-and-hollows field. It belongs, the field, to the next-door farmer, and once there must have been a house, for the wide, square moat is still there, with the island in the middle, just enough higher than the fields around to keep it clear of floods when the stream overflows. But of the house itself, not a brick nor tile to be found, for we have often searched, the children and I, all of us haunted a little by the vanished presence.

It must have been made of pressed mud thatched with straw, like much old local building. "Cob" they call it here, and it gives the cottages a gentle rounded shape, so that the village streets have the oddest air of being children's toys, and it is hard to believe that people do anything as serious in them as earning their living, much less dying.

Cob cottages are warm and dry while they are looked after, warmer far than our thin shell of bricks and glass, but, once neglected, as our house was for years, they crumble back into the soil they came from, leaving only these irregular hummocks in the field, where the children play Hide and Seek. I try vainly to arrange the ridges into a plan of rooms, but it is no good. They are too irregular and too small, even remembering that rooms half-built on their foundations always do look quite absurdly small. Just as any room seems smaller if you look at the ceiling. It is how I encourage myself with the spring-cleaning: sit back and look at the ceiling, and think that really, if the room is no bigger than *that*, I can easily distemper it in a morning, even if the children do insist on "helping."

But the humps-and-hollows house can never have compared with this. For this house, although it is no more than a largish farm, has the same delightful intimacy controlled by dignity as Hampton Court. And, living here alone these last war years with the children while their father is away, my closest companion has been the man who built it, four centuries ago.

"What I do is me: for that I came," says Hopkins, and this house is what my builder did, dealt out "that being indoors each one dwells," a self of natural dignity, a serene mind, and intense but quite unselfconscious charm.

He chose his site because of the stream, one supposes, for it never runs dry in the longest drought. He dug out the encircling moat and piled it up as an island to build his house on against the damp and floods. Then the house itself, this arrangement of wood and bricks and plaster, which, like the great works of art, is so overwhelmingly more than the sum of its parts.

Living in it, I am sure that it was designed, not from outside like most houses, but from the inside, and by the person who was to make his life in it. Most houses are moulds into which the rooms are made to fit, none more so than the eighteenth-century mansions; but here each room is built for itself, is made the size and shape and height for the life to be lived in it. So that every room has its own personality, some low-ceilinged and snug for the Winter, with long, wide windows, some with arched, airy ceilings up to the roof, and cool oak floors. And yet from outside the irregular units of rooms compose quite simply into an L-shaped whole of curiously organic beauty, as the Gothic churches grow together all their odd additions. And inside there is an intellectual order more satisfying than any symmetry. For coming in at the front door, one sees at once the whole plan of living: the long hall through to the square kitchen, the facing staircase, and the rooms opening off each side.

Everywhere there are windows, their old panes as thin as wineglasses, two windows for most rooms, four in the great kitchen, and all facing the sun, for the north of the house is pantries and storerooms and a long paved dairy where the children keep their larger toys. He loved light and sunshine, my builder, as he must have hated dark corners and passages and awkward steps. For here there are no steps at all, not even to the front door, and the children can ride their tricycles round the kitchen, down the hall, out on to the lawn and back again, without getting off. But the inside doors are scarcely wide enough for tricycles, which need a wide clearance as ridden by small children. The doors indeed must have been awkwardly narrow both for farthingales and crinolines, even though people were smaller then, when these doors were built, and there is scarcely one I can go through without stooping. But then crinolines certainly, and perhaps farthingales too, never can have been the enormous bells the painters show us, for no ordinary Victorian doorway is wide enough to let them pass.

Perhaps it is only a sentimental invention of our synthetic century that we imagine the old builders deliberately respecting their materials. If our beams (a wealth of old oak, as the house-agents say) are shaped with an adze and pegged with wood, it is perhaps only because there were no screws or circular saws. But still I hope not. For the tool marks on the wood, so hard now that it bends the nails I try to hammer in, the irregular marks of the adze bring us as close to the long-dead workmen as Rubens is close to us in the brilliant brushwork of his painting.

This house is a great frame of split oak trees filled in with bricks, a way of building which must leave much freedom in the planning. The bricks are smaller than any we use now, crumbling and uneven, of a soft plant-pot red splotched with yellow lichen, with here and there little lozenge patterns of shiny darker bricks. In the kitchen and at the back door the beams are left rough, still in the curved shapes they grew in the tree, and the unplastered bricks show through the distemper like thread in rough linen. But in the nursery, which would be the best parlour if we lived a best-parlour life, the stone frame of the inglenook is carved in a wide perpendicular arch, with the great cross-beams of the ceiling moulded to match. And on the staircase the oak heads of the newel-posts are cut in facets like gems, so that it is an intimate and familiar pleasure to feel the smooth edges turning under your hand as you swing round at the bottom.

Like the Gothic churches, too, the house is full of inconsequential delights. There are deep cupboards in unexpected places, there is a ceiling which curves into the wall like a rounded saucepan, there is a bedroom floor so sloping that a cot will run from one side to the other (the children's pleasure, this), and there is even a secret room opening off my bedroom chimney. But I have never been inside, preferring the secret to the inevitable dust.

When builders design houses now, I wonder if they know how much it matters that doors and windows should be so arranged that we can see right through the house and out beyond. Making of it not a box-like prison, but, as this house is, a light and airy shell to shelter in from the weather.

But the essential poetry of the house cannot be deliberate. No one could *plan* to build such strangely moving beauty. The beauty must come unsought, like happiness, as a by-product, "as kingfishers catch fire." For this house is so intensely itself that if it were pulled down and scattered over the countryside, I think I should know, five fields away, each separate brick.

This, for the children when they draw, is always their idea of "House." Not the usual roofed cube with a central chimney and *clouds* of smoke, but strange, valiant attempts at foreshortening this L-shaped mass with its lovely uneven roofs. They have worked out an unlikely-looking formula which they both accept, just as their agreed sign for station is a zigzag line, because our local lamp-lit station has a pie-crust cut-out edging to the roofs over the platforms. No buildings, no railway lines, simply a zigzag line, and that means station.

WE have been to the circus, and ever since we came back the children have tumbled about deliriously being clowns. For they like the clowns best, and the horses least, and the only thing which impressed them about the lions and tigers were the precautions considered necessary before they were let loose. "They're *very* fierce. Look at all those railings."

Really most of a circus seems to be coaxing unlikely animals to do with difficulty what the proper ones do without thinking. Strong men struggle to lift weights while elephants shuffle on their hind legs. Girls swing on trapezes and monkeys drink cups of tea. Men dive into water-tanks and seals balance balls on their noses.

Still, there are a lot of things I would not miss. I like the smell. I like the way the lions and tigers sit on their stools and yawn, as if at some excruciatingly dull tea-party. I like the embarrassed man who shovels up the gargantuan elephant droppings. I like the great dapple-grey horse, with a back as broad as the deck of a ship, who canters round and round in serene indifference to the pink and gold ladies who pirouette on his back. Then, always, in the middle of the juggler, I am suddenly over-come with astonishment at the human animal, not that a man should be able to balance a teacup on a spoon on the end of his nose, but that he should *want* to, that he should ever think of doing it.

Best of all are the bears, for whenever I go to a circus

the bears run amuck. Once they broke their leads and shuffled firmly back to their cages. Once, but luckily they were small ones, they turned on their keepers in a fury. Today they simply sat down and growled, a friendly-sounding noise, though I can hardly think it was meant to be. Certainly whenever I am at the circus the bears never perform, but only demonstrate against such a parody of their natural dignity.

John has already chosen his future career. When he grows up he is going to tame wild animals. The circus has finally decided it, but he has always been fond of what he calls his Taming.

JOHN: "Rabbits are very shy. They won't let you pick them up."

PETER: "No. Bulls are more shyest. You mustn't even go into the field where bulls are. They don't like it."

I often eavesdrop at the nursery door as I pass, but it is not often so rewarding.

Taming rabbits John has sadly given up, though he once had ambitious plans for digging pits in the front meadow. "I know where the paths are that they go on," he said, so he would dig holes here and there, and the rabbits were to fall obligingly in. "And then I can pick them up from their ears, like they pick white ones up." But he has given up rabbits now and resigned himself to beetles, which are much easier to catch, he finds. Carefully he lines a matchbox with leaves and half fills it with cake crumbs. Bread, he thinks, is not good enough. We always give visitors cake, he says, so his beetle must have cake too. Then he finds a poor wretched beetle, and in it goes. His Wrecky Animal he calls it, hearing me call it wretched, and not knowing what it means. "I'm going to find a Wrecky Animal to tame it," he says, going off with his matchbox.

He leaves it shut up for a time, "to get used to his nice new house, and have a *good* dinner." And after that the Taming begins. He opens the box warily and the anxious creature comes hurrying out. "*Dear* beetle. *Nice* beetle. Don't go away. I love you *very* much. Look." And he strokes it firmly, breaking its legs.

This goes on until the poor insect is too battered and exhausted even to try to escape, and John is satisfied at last. "There. Now it's a tame beetle. Not a Wrecky Animal. Now it won't go away and leave me," and back it goes into the matchbox prison. "It lives with me now. It's my *nice* little beetle."

He looks at it a dozen times an hour, and gives it biscuit crumbs. "Perhaps it's tired of cake." He puts it carefully on the windowsill by his bed for the night. "It will get squashed under my pillow," he says. And in the morning it is always dead, upside down with its bent legs in the air. For small dead animals are always pathetically on their backs, flies and birds and fishes.

I have watched John torture the creature to death with great cruelty, and said not a word to stop him. Because he meant it in all kindness, and because the death of an occasional beetle seems a small price to pay for the exercise of his loving heart. But man is a complicated new animal when his simplest decisions carry such metaphysical implications.

And John is sad but resigned. "Beetles don't live long. Beetles always die. They don't eat enough dinner. Rabbits are better."

WHEN we first read the case-histories of Havelock Ellis, they are of enthralling interest. "Here," we think, "is what I shall read now always, everything else is superficial." But how very quickly we are bored, how soon they seem only stale and squalid and, above all, *dull*. We end by feeling, not that neurosis is a fascinating country, but that to explore at such length these small, self-centred, and essentially un-original minds must be the most boring branch of all medicine. Not for a doctor perhaps, for he is studying the disease and not the people, but certainly for us.

Which I think is one of the reasons why the arts so fail to satisfy when the artists—painters, writers, composers—are looking only inward at themselves. Not at the world reflected in their own unique mind (that is what the great artists do, and quite a different matter), but at themselves. For a great deal of modern art is really elaborated case-histories, and though it has a first quick interest, it does not last. For however brilliant a man's mind may be, however fascinating an exploration for himself, it can never compare with the outside world in complexity and range and meaning. There is simply not enough in any single mind to be satisfying, we *must* see the world through it as well.

So since it seems that modern writers will not do to escape the Winter claustrophobia of the house, I have been reading the weather books instead. It is exhilarating, after a day in the kitchen, to be whirled up thousands of feet to the top of a thundercloud, to be blown with the winds which sweep across the upper atmosphere, carrying back the air displaced on the surface of the world by the earthly winds we know. It is fascinating to think of air as if it were water, as the weather books do, air flowing down from the cold hills at night, forming in pools against impeding walls and hedges, until it overflows them and slides on to collect in a lake in the valley, killing the tender plants of any gardener who is ill-advised enough to make his garden in a hollow between hills.

The simpler astronomers too, for the advanced ones are really too difficult, breaking out in mathematical formulæ as if they were bursting into song; but the simpler ones are an even more complete escape, leaving the world so far behind that we lose sight of the entire human race. And reading them, skipping the figures, we catch for a moment their conception of a universe, not of solid matter, but of a vast pattern of inter-acting orbits.

To the layman the universe is static. The earth is solidly here, the stars there, and nothing much changes except a certain wheeling round of the stars, useful for finding our way at night, if we only knew how. So that the questions we naturally ask—what the stars are made of, what is inside the earth—are not the questions the astronomers seem most concerned with. It is as if we saw, so ephemeral we are, only an instantaneous snap-shot of fast traffic, showing a random group of unrelated motor-cars. So that what we want to know is not where they are going, since we cannot tell from our photograph that they are going anywhere, but who is in them, and what they are. But to the astronomers watching the real traffic of astronomical time, it is the movement which matters, the speed and direction and interaction, a universe not of inert matter but of forces.

Yet books are books still, even about winds and stars, and we are all heartily tired of the house. We can only look sadly at the hills, which seem so far away in bad weather. For the hills are more themselves in Winter, and live with an intenser secret life. In Summer they are part of our everyday background, a familiar backdrop for domesticity. As we lie in the buttercups they are a long, wavy horizon through the stalks, the constant boundary of our view, an incitement to expeditions on fine days when I ought to do the washing. By August they have grown almost domestic, and on fine Sundays we think we can even make out the picnic parties, dotted about among the dotted juniper bushes.

But now in Winter we live sheltered in the house, and only come upon the hills crossing the orchard to fetch the milk from the farm, remote, self-sufficient, another country. For they are rainy when we are fine, bright with silvery light when we are dull, white with snow and looking like mountains, secret in their mist for days together. And *far* too cold for picnics.

So I can only look instead at the reproduction of Renoir's *Parapluies* which I found in the National Gallery one day when I was Christmas-shopping in London. I brought it home to pin on the kitchen wall, and now, whenever I feel too shut in this gloomy introspective Winter, I look at it and take myself to France. For it is only in France, I suppose because it is the only Latin country I know, that I can live so directly through the senses, short-circuiting the tiresome mind. In front of the wonderful Renoir of the luncheon-party I feel myself change to a different sort of person, living as perhaps the wise do, intensely in the moment.

Yet it is not exactly mindless pleasure, this delight in sheeny silk and light reflected upwards on to faces, in the expansiveness of warm air, and mottled sun through leaves. But still it is independent of the synthesizing mind, which needs to see the whole pattern of one's life in every smallest occasion. And this gift of Renoir's, for making ordinary life delicious, is for me quite un-English. Here, if we have it at all, it is in the working-class, the most cosmopolitan of our people. But it needs more sun than we ever have in this rainbow island half-way to the North Pole.

Renoir paints with soft outlines and tenderly, but quite

without romanticism or sentimentality, an attitude too mature for any northerner; as if people, like peaches, needed sun to ripen them. And, like all the best things in modern French culture, he is a bourgeois painter. *"La Cuisine Bourgeoise,"* they say proudly of the world's best cooking, for the French know very well where their greatness lies. He is for the middle-aged too, not for the young. For what does youth, living through the mind and the emotions, know of this direct and untroubled delight in warmth and colour, the taste of peaches and the touch of silk and velvet?

So there it lives, my *Parapluies*. A rainy day of black frocks and umbrellas, yet it glows with delight on the kitchen wall. And I have fallen completely in love with the young girl in the middle. Not the serious brown-eyed child with the hoop, for she is a long-standing passion, but the girl who is no more than a chin and the softest of creamy necks.

John, when he was younger, had the same sort of deliciousness, so that, like Renoir's children, one really wanted to eat him. His skin was always soft and firm with a faint flowery smell (was it Alexander who smelt of violets?), and his breath was sweet like cows' breath after hay.

Well, he is like that no longer. Now he is quite simply dirty the whole time. This afternoon he came in so grey all over with dust from the chaff that only his eyes showed white, like a nervous horse. He had been playing in the great barn at the other side of the cow-yard. It was built in the sixteenth century, at the same time as this farmhouse, and is twice as big. The brick filling between the beams has been replaced by weather boarding, the tile roof by russet-painted corrugated iron, but inside the great arched scaffolding of oak is still as solid as ever.

And here "when the Eastern blasts prove very tedious," as John Evelyn would say, I take the children to play in shelter. It is always half dark, for the windows are high and cobwebby, but that is part of its fascination, that and the rich mixed smell of corn and animals and earth floor. At one end are the calves born last Autumn and too young still for the open yard, a row of curious heads watching us over their dividing manger. In the middle there is the cross-bar which works the electrical tools, a mill for oats, a machine which chops up turnips, a circular saw. Whenever the children hear the hum of the motor, they drop their toys, squeeze through the bars of the gate, pick their way between the cows and dung-heaps in the yard, and go to find out what is happening.

There are piles of corn waiting for the mill, where they bury each other in smooth, cool graves, and fling themselves down from the highest sack shouting: "Look how high *I* can jump." Sometimes, when the Farmer is there, they are permitted to pour the corn into the mill, or fetch empty sacks from the other barn, or feed the calves with hay. And, busy and important, they come and tell me of their labours, proud to feel they have been running the farm single-handed.

Here today I left them playing under the eye of the cowman while I cycled the six miles or so to fetch the rations. But how I hate cycling in Winter, windy and cold, using only a few prescribed muscles in an arrangement like a treadmill, so that one is not even taking exercise, but drearily producing horse-power. Yet I once cycled round Denmark for fun. But then one has to cycle in Denmark, not only because everyone else does, but because it really is too small for motor-cars, too unemphatic. And although the buses are charming and friendly and will sling your bicycle on to the roof when you are tired, they do limit the number of ice-creams you can eat at the wayside stalls, *real* ice-cream with cream and nuts and honey. In Copenhagen the fleets of bicycles curve and interlace like the patterns of an intricate ballet, delicately in this delicate city, where the very air seems thinner than in the south. The light is cool and clear, and everywhere the sea flows in canals between the buildings, green as the green copper roofs and the dragons writhing so surprisingly up the spire of the Bourse.

And always, even at midsummer, you feel the threat of the long Winter, the true climate. All the doors and windows are double, gardening must be done indoors in pots on walls and windowsills, and between the fields of blond corn, rows of dark fir trees are planted as wind-breaks, giving the open rolling country a curious park-like air. So that you know you must not loiter, but travel south unhesitating with the Summer birds, or you too will be overtaken by the Arctic night, imprisoned in darkness. In the Winter the Danes skate across the frozen tideless Baltic to Sweden. And once, so they told me, the cold came so quickly that it froze the swans in solid as they sat on the Gulf of Copenhagen.

It has been another dark, wet day, with the children more than ever tiresome, and I am depressed by the thought of how many more hundreds of days there must be before they grow into reasonable beings. But at least they are no longer babies, which is the first and greatest improvement, for even after my own, I like babies no better than I ever did.

They are born far too soon. Not, of course, for the sailing, impatient mothers-to-be, but for good taste. For the first few months they are less like human beings than precocious fœtuses. The only thing to do is to look after

them, since one must, but thinking hard and hopefully of
grown-up schoolboys in caps. Yet we surround them
with a fantastically unsuitable aura of ribbons and pretti-
ness; lace and gossamer shawls for growing animals
which thrive with almost frightening vigour in their self-
made habitat of squalor. For they are quite astonishingly
vigorous, and certainly need to be to survive the varying
and contradictory fashions of baby-care.

One loves them, of course, would make any sacrifice
for them, is sick with apprehension when they are ill,
would probably die for them. Not at all heroically, not
even as a conscious choice, for of course it is easier to
make new babies than new mothers, but simply as a
maternal animal. For a species whose young are so long
helpless could scarcely have survived till now without
evolving the fiercest mother-love for the newly born.

At the time it is all-engrossing, but then so is the tooth-
ache, and of no more relevance to one's individual self.
It is like an extreme climate to which one's character is
exposed, and we adapt ourselves to suit it, grow more
self-controlled, more tolerant, less selfish. Like an east
wind in Spring, it prunes away the more self-centred
absurdities, so that at least I have no time now to sit
weighing shadows as I used to, left alone. "Children are
a kind of discipline of humanity," Bacon said (and he
included wives as well), but there are so many disciplines
in being a parent besides the obvious ones like getting up
in the night and putting up with the noise in the day.
And almost the hardest of all is learning to be a well of
affection and not a fountain, to show them we love them,
not when *we* feel like it, but when *they* do.

When John runs to tell me excited stories, or Peter is
endearingly practising his formal manners, I must never,
never interrupt to love them, but somehow learn to store

it in a common pool of affection for when they want it:
for when Peter climbs silently on to my knee, always
when I am most in a hurry, or John in the middle of my
baking-day comes to me sobbing: "I'm not very happy.
Not happy at *all*." For they are defenceless, as all children are, against the sudden griefs of childhood, like
coming on a nettle where we thought there were only
flowers.

The times they come for my affection are almost never
the times I want to show it. But it is always one of the
tragedies of any relationship, even between people sensitive to each other's moods, that the moments of emotion
so rarely coincide.

Waking up these dismal mornings to the hungry children and the fires to light, I sit on the edge of the bed,
and shudder at the cold, and say to comfort myself:
"Now is the Winter of my discontent," and I sigh to
start another day. Not every morning certainly, but
rather like the curate's egg. From the children's rooms I
hear them calling to each other: "Let's go Moling. Come
on." It is one of their favourite games to play in bed.
"Let's go Moling," they shout, for children never talk
but shout always, and down they burrow to the bottom
of their beds. And hearing them I sigh, knowing it will
take twice as long to make the beds that morning. Sometimes, instead of moles they are worms, "Snakes" they
call it, but whichever it is, the beds are just as chaotic at
the end.

This morning I found them both in Peter's bed. They
had never thought of doing it before, and found it an
uproarious joke. "Look," they said between giggles,
"two people in one bed. Like two feet in one shoe."

Sitting on the bed listening to their bouncing and
shouting, I imagine mornings of remote perfection, of

waking in Summer to Mozart's music in a room looking over the gardens of Saint-Cloud. Well, when it is all over, this wholesome backwoods pioneering in family life, when the children are young minds to explore instead of young animals to look after, then we will all have a serene high drawing-room of grey and white, and the country-dance movements in Haydn's quartets shall be our nearest approach to the simple life. Flowers shall be cut from their roots, and forget, in china vases, the soil they thrived in, and even the pot-plants shall sprout discreetly from jardinieres. I will play at the country-life like Marie Antoinette at the Petit Trianon, and do my gardening from indoors, with a toy trowel in window-boxes. But not yet. Here I go round with a hook in Summer and slash back the waves of green, nettles and willow-herb and elderberry, a sea which creeps up constantly from the orchard to engulf us. And I mow the lawns, not from neatness, but so that the children shall have somewhere smooth to play when the orchard grass meets above their heads.

Living so far from the village the children run wild, and I struggle to teach them formal manners out here where there are so few formal occasions. Yet if they are to meet people without knowing the expected gestures, how can they help being awkward, like going to a ball without knowing how to dance? So, quite simply, I introduce them to everyone who comes near us, the men who bring the coal, the men who collect the tins, the threshers, the hay-makers, the vanman who fetches the cows for market, all the people who come and go on a busy farm. "I shall introduce you," I say, coaching them every time I see someone coming through the orchard to the house, "and you will shake hands and say: 'How do you do.'" They think it is an odd game of the grown-ups', and are delighted that they know how to play it too.

The butcher and baker and candlestick-maker are generally quite unconscious that they are taking part in a formal ceremony. But the children are determined to play their game thoroughly. If no hand is offered them, they hunt round purposefully till they find one, pulling it out of pockets if need be, holding it firmly in either or both of their own, left or right, whichever is nearer, holding it simply, as if they were going for a walk. "How do you do. How do you do." They say it confidently, needing no answer.

But really the children could have no better example of natural good manners than the Farmer they spend so much of their time with. He seldom shaves or wears a collar except on market-days, his accent is as thick as the heavy clay land he farms, and he is a very prince of courtesy. I have never known him behave awkwardly, never say the wrong thing or appear self-conscious. He talks to everyone with the same quiet dignity, from Lord X, who is his landlord, to the cowman, who swears as naturally as breathing. Watching him, one feels there are no difficulties in social contacts, no pitfalls or embarrassments, it is all quite simple and inevitable. But it is a rare gift, this natural grace which can make its own manners for any occasion, and one notices it most often in uneducated people. But perhaps only because it is then so obviously their own personal tact, owing nothing to formal behaviour.

There is another natural paragon in the local town. He is the man who lifts things about at the weekly auction sales. "Lot 61," the auctioneer calls, and my friend holds it up for all to see. "Here it is. A coal-scuttle, a coffee-grinder, and a pair of Wellington boots." He buys things for me, since I have no time to go and bid for myself, and I meet him often, wheeling his hand-cart of furniture about the streets.

I get off my bicycle, and he sets down his cart. I ask him how his eel-traps are doing, for fishing is his delight, and he tells me little stories of the sale-room which is his small peculiar world. For a long time I have wanted to introduce him to the Farmer, for the pleasure of watching two such princes converse.

Then there was a French postman I once knew in Paris who had the same natural courtesy. He would call for me before his round, at a quite distressingly early hour, and take me to see Les Halles at work. For this, he said, was a side of Paris very few visitors ever see, and small wonder either, since one must get up at five in the morning to see it. And he would show me with pride the great busy markets, for he had the entrée everywhere, greeting his friends at every corner.

The French working-class, at least the older ones and the peasants of the south, have a tradition of formal manners which we know nothing of. To watch two families meet and greet each other in the streets of Arles, exchange civilities, and take leave again—this is a very lesson in deportment. And if one sits down for lunch with the man who drives the cart across the Camargue, there will be no awkwardness on either side. He is the perfect host, just suitably formal, but easy, gay, and with a fund of amusing small talk which never interferes with the serious pleasure of eating.

But good manners, like good cooking, seem only to be achieved by long civilization. In the south of France one is always conscious that their culture has been unbroken back to Roman times and beyond, that they were savouring their wine and behaving gracefully at ceremonies when we were still crude barbarians huddled in wretched huts.

My only comfort is that so far the children are not shy. It is an infection which they have managed until now not to catch.

JOHN: "What does shy mean?"

PETER: "Shy is when little girls hide against their mother. And they won't talk. And if you talk to them they laugh. And then they cry. I don't know why they do it. And that's called shy."

So it is, and the simplest way of dealing with it is to treat them as they treat each other, which is not in the least the way one manages a shy grown-up. Small children, even the shyest, do not seem to mind in the least being looked at. One can stare and stare without at all upsetting them, but only so long as it is blankly and in silence. That is their own method, and they seem quite indifferent to its embarrassments. But any sign of a closer approach sends them diving into their mother's skirts like ostriches. One must not, as Peter noticed, say hello, however encouragingly. Must not fill with bright chatter what seems an awkward moment to a grown-up. And above all, one must not smile at them, for that, it seems, is the most alarming approach of all.

One must stare simply, with a completely noncommittal face, then turn away and do something else. And when they feel safe enough, they will come up and stare in their turn. And after a time, reassured (and perhaps piqued too, who knows?) by such mild indifference, they will join in too, and talk, and forget that they were shy. Only one must not notice them, must not look straight at them, must not talk to them directly, for their new self-assurance is as tender as the horns of cockled snails, and anything which makes them self-conscious again sends them back into their shell.

"How I wish I had the other reel of cotton," one can sigh to the ceiling. Or: "I *would* like the scissors I left on the kitchen table." And off they rush without a word to fetch them, bringing them back, beaming with pride and pleasure, delighted to do a grown-up a service. And, like the rest of us, they seem paradoxically to love us, not for the good we do them, but for the good they do us, feeling perhaps that our goodwill must be real because they have earned it. So that half a dozen simple wishes sighed into thin air for them to act fairy godmother, and they are our friends for good.

I often wonder how children arrive at their judgements about people, judgements which seem to have so little to do with presented fact. There is a character in one of Giraudoux's plays, I think it is Helen in *La Guerre de Troie n'aura pas lieu*. She imagines the future, and if the picture is black and white she knows it will not happen, if it is coloured it is true. It need not be quite like that, though we must have some private way of assessing the inner person behind the front he shows us. But we can think of him behaving in some imagined situation— the seeming-brave man behaving as a coward; the coward managing somehow desperately to be a hero; the honest cheating in the dark; the ruthless checked by unexpected scruples. And sometimes the picture is so vividly real that we know beyond any doubt that is how they would behave. It is some pointless habitual gesture, perhaps, which in the next context of imagined action reveals its true meaning, some tone of voice which before was only odd but is now significant. It is as if they showed us, in conscious meetings, only a façade hiding the building behind. But we can say hello against them, and listen for the echoes which come back, not only from the façade, but if we listen carefully, from all the hidden rooms beyond. And, because it has nothing to do with their conscious behaviour or with our logical judgement, the unconscious deception we all practise on each other has no place, nor have our own errors of reasoning. So that if we have such a vividly imagined picture of any person, it is seldom mistaken, however unlikely it may seem at first. As we get to know them closely, we shall find in time the rooms the echo came from, the faults they would conceal, the virtues they are shy about, however carefully they may be hidden behind the façade.

Perhaps in some dim way, for it is impossible to know, this is how children judge the people they meet, and why they take such seemingly irrational fancies or dislikes.

Meeting new people for the first time, there is sometimes a lightning vision of what their relationship with us might be. It may be pleasant or hostile, intimate or formal, but in the very first moment there is this sudden knowledge of what there could be between us. It has nothing to do with foreseeing the future or with Mr. Dunne's theory of time, for it may never happen. We may say polite how-do-you-do's and never meet again. It is only a sudden vista of potentialities. Seeing a seedling, one can tell at once whether it will grow into an oak tree or a daisy, but not whether it will live or die. It is an instantaneous vision, quickly fading. After the first meeting one's contact is limited to ordinary progressive acquaintance, the inherent possibilities half forgotten and overlaid by accepted fact.

* * *

WINTER

ALL day the children have been painting on the nursery floor, with big brushes, and jars of poster-paints, and sheets of shelf paper big enough to wrap themselves in.

I daresay they would rather colour the pictures in their reading books as I used to do, carefully, with a hair-thin brush and my nose on the page, boasting that I had never gone over the line, not *once*. But it is not fashionable any longer to let the young paint neatly. Nowadays they must splash and daub. To keep inside the line is to be inhibited, that dreadful thing, and nothing will do but a Picassoish freedom. How absurdly earnest we all are now with our poor children. And it makes no difference in the end. If they are splashers and daubers, they splash and daub, and if they are not, they still manage to paint neatly, however enormous the paper or clumsy the brush. Peter simply divides off a small area of the sheet and paints his tidy Paul Kleeish pictures inside it, trains and trees and lorries and houses, neatly fitted into each other's angles and into the border of the picture. But the fashionable freehand suits John. Even his half-inch brush today seem too fiddling, so he emptied the paint-jars into the middle of his paper and spread them round with his hand.

JOHN: "Do you like my picture?"

ME: "That's not a picture, that's a mess."

JOHN: "Yes, a mess. But a picture as well. It's the inside of a hill."

ME: "Yes. Why don't you do it with mud, outside on the concrete?"

JOHN: "Yes," thoughtfully. "Yes," with growing enthusiasm. "Yes," with delighted conviction. "I can paint hills all down the path. All the way to the stream."

So now he plays his usual game of mud puddles to please himself, and calls them hill-pictures to please the grown-ups, and everyone is happy except Peter, who is a fastidious creature and does not like the mess on the path.

But Peter's painting just now is always the same. He paints the Night Engine. It is high romance, it is passion, it is everything strange and beautiful, the love of his life. For he sits and paints in dreamy concentration, sheet after sheet. A background of deep purplish-blue, with a pale-coloured haze like a more romantic Turner, and dissolved in the haze, the central undefined mystery, is the Night Engine.

The Night Engine, he says, sleeps all day in a tall, leafy tree, and I have never risked not being told another word by asking how it gets there. It only comes out at night, and even so, not just any night, but only on very special occasions. It rushes round the countryside with a strange roaring noise, he says, and has lots and lots of bright lights, which change colour all the time without anyone doing anything about it. It has no carriages, it never stops, and only special people can see it. He thinks I might be able to, though he is not sure. John can only see it on certain days, when they have not quarrelled.

I look at Peter's radiant clouds and think I will show him Turner. But perhaps not. For should we offer children the big experiences (though, for that matter, Turner is not at all my own fancy, and I doubt whether Peter would consider his pictures any better than his own achievements in the same genre), but should children be offered anything when they are too young to take it in? Should we give them Shakespeare to read at school, and send them abroad, and take them to concerts, and trail them round the picture galleries? It is hard to know. The things which impress us young impress us most permanently, but still there is only one first time for everything, and if it comes before we are ready, we can never afterwards feel that brilliant shock of pleasure at suddenly discovering the new and unimagined experience.

We should visit countries in their stormy seasons. I forget who said it, but he said it in French, and by *"orageux"* I think he meant, not so much stormy, as in their seasons of excess: Provence at blazing midsummer, Norway in the Arctic night, and England, I suppose, since we are only excessive in our mildness, some soft green Winter day.

It is true of countries, but just as true of writers and painters and the rest. We should take a good big bite of their strongest flavour while they are still a new excitement to our unaccustomed palate. Jump straight in the deep end of the pool with *The Golden Bowl*, Turner's emptiest canvases, Beethoven's late quartets, El Greco's most passionate distortions. We never get the full flavour if we first take homeopathic doses of their milder creations until we scarcely notice the individual taste.

We must jump in and drown, and when we come out at the other side, our once familiar world will be changed, will be mysterious with new subtleties, unexpected implications. Every face in the street, even somehow the fat ones, is narrow and mournful after Modigliani, the apples on the table are cosmically significant after Cézanne.

They change back in time, of course, to ordinary apples, ordinary faces, but never quite so ordinary again. Some faint shadow of the strangeness will always be there, because we ourselves have changed.

I saw *Sylphides* as my very first ballet somewhere in my schooldays, a travelling company, I suppose, in our northern town, and I drowned utterly. I had never dreamed that such a world of grace existed anywhere, that the everyday human body could create such magic.

I remember still my great gasp of pleasure when the hero jumped for the first time, rose without any effort at all, soared straight for the ceiling against all the laws of gravity. For it seemed then a quite enormous leap, as if he never would come down again. I was even too engrossed to spare more than a moment for embarrassment when the row in front of me in the theatre turned round to stare at my gasping enthusiasm.

For days after, I went about in a dream of dancing. The people in the streets, pathetic, stunted people of a depressed area, clumsy with heavy work—even these sad figures were transformed because of *Sylphides*. And since everything which has moved us deeply becomes part of our consciousness for the rest of our lives, the magic has never quite gone. Sometimes a turn of the head will bring it back, a hand's gesture, the smooth way a girl stoops to pick up a fallen letter, a young man walking proud and straight across the street. Even the tired housewives waiting in queues in their enveloping dingy clothes, even still they rouse faint echoes of that other world, suggest remembered attitudes of grace. For all movements of all human beings are more beautiful because of *Sylphides*, as all human minds are nobler because of La Place de la Concorde.

But some things we see far too soon for them to make any impression. Classical sculpture, for instance, we all see when we are too young for any other reaction than a mild surprise at so many grown-up people standing about with no clothes on in the cold. All the Classical culture comes too soon, for how can we help it when it is the tradition we are brought up in? But it makes it the hardest of all for us to appreciate freshly. It is so much the air we breathe that it has no smell to our accustomed nostrils, no more flavour than water. Not in the least because it is insipid, but because, as Europeans, we have been taught to see the world like this. Our conception of man and society seems to us an abstract reality, not the highly specialized vision of one particular culture, which it is. It is the other conceptions which for us are the distortions, however beautiful—the Egyptian, the Indian, the Chinese—these are the individual flavours, ours is simple, matter-of-fact. So walking through the Classical sculpture in the Louvre, we are struck, not by the conceptions of the artists, but by their skill and power. "Yes," we feel (natural modesty being rare as the Phœnix), "that is how *I* should show men and women if I were an artist, that is quite superbly what sculpture *should* be like." But none the less, apart from the early Greek and the *Winged Victory*, we are bored.

For the proper way to go to the Louvre is to go first to the Pre-Columbian art at the Musée de l'Homme, the Aztecs, Incas, Mayas, and all the other ancient civilizations of America which I can never remember. Here is a world of evil magic. Life is cruel and inexplicable. Man has no power over his own destiny, and can only hope to survive by horrible sacrifices to pitiless gods. After this dark and fearful world of cruelty and terror, we see the Classical sculpture for what it really is, a vision of men as radiant god-like creatures. They are not frightened. Their attitudes are noble and beautiful, easy yet controlled. They live in a sunlit world of serene dignity and clear-minded truth.

Well, it seems a long way from any conscious conception we have of ourselves, but until we are surprised by Classical sculpture (which we never are except by the hermaphrodites), it must still subconsciously be what we believe.

In any case, the Classical periods, ancient or modern,

are not for children. They are not only too adult, but too complicated. The Middle Ages are more sympathetic to a child's mind, and simpler, because they have no background of a wider culture, as Classical art has always— Renaissance paintings, Adam buildings, eighteenth-century literature. In the Middle Ages there are fewer echoes and implications, only the thing itself, the picture or story or poem. It is as if the northern barbarians, destroying Rome, cut themselves off from the classical civilization which was to be their ultimate background, and their culture flowed as a local stream, until it joined the main river at the Renaissance.

ALL night the cows were restless in the yard, lowing and calling, but I never got up to look. Knowing even in my sleep that only babies are my business, I never properly awoke. But small wonder they had a troubled night, for this morning their sheds were flooded, the yard under water, and the wretched animals marooned on the dungheap.

The view is quite astonishingly different, for we are an island in a swirling, foaming, threatening brown sea. "Horseback brown," Hopkins called it, and so it is, and just as solid-looking. Judging by the drowned trees, the water can be no more than two feet or so deep, but it might as well be full fathom five, for it is just as convincing a deluge. We are cut off from the farm by a roaring river sweeping over our shaky little bridge (the hand-rail has gone already), and the miserable unmilked cows are cut off with us, crowding on to their tiny hill, watching this visitation with pained surprise.

All morning the water has been rising round the house, deep in the moat, drowning the hedges, rising in contours up the lawn, which shows as uneven as a natural pearl for all my rolling. And for the first time I wish we had steps to the doors. I sit like Canute and watch the advancing tide, and wonder whether I must carry the rugs and books and furniture upstairs. "When the water reaches the children's sand-pit," I tell myself, "then I will start."

The children are horribly excited, John not knowing whether it is more fun or frightening, but Peter quite decided. He has taken all his toys up to his bedroom, and is sitting on the top step of the staircase, waiting for death by drowning. Nothing I can say to reassure him really offsets the water creeping up every hour round the house.

By evening our flood was over. Peter was coaxed down for lunch by promises of being carried back upstairs if the water came into the house, and then rescued by boat from the bedroom window as they do in stories. All right, he said, but he would like his Wellington boots on before he came downstairs, and to wear them all the time for lunch. He will be fastidious even in his dying, it seems.

But after lunch the water was going down again without ever quite reaching us, which is what I had all the time expected, such trust I have in my friend who built this house. And by tea-time the cowman could paddle across to his unhappy cows, and we could all paddle across to the farm, and the children tell the Farmer in high, excited voices, Did he know? But we'd had a *flood!* As if he might not have noticed it for himself. By evening it was all over, and nothing left of our astonishing sea but a layer of black silt over lawns and flower-beds, a mulch to delight any gardener. And since Peter felt he had been saved from a watery death, and even John was relieved, we all ate an enormous high tea to celebrate our deliverance, and read *Mrs. Tittlemouse* by the nursery fire. Of all the Beatrix Potter books, the children love *Mrs. Tittlemouse* the best. To begin with, it is one of the few I have managed to find in English, most of them (it seems an odd sidelight on world war) being in French. *Poupette-à-l'Épingle* for *Mrs. Tiggy-Winkle*, *Noisy-Noisette* for *Squirrel Nutkin*. I translate for them (Squirrel Nutkin's riddles are almost too much for me), but they are impatient that it does not come the same each time, word for word, as they like it to be. So they prefer *Mrs. Tittlemouse*, who is in English, and who is, moreover, an old friend. For she is the mouse we catch in our traps, the inhabitant of the dolls'-house, with her dead friends and relations. And, like Beatrix Potter, the children have always found her "a most terribly tidy particular little mouse." Especially she is tidy, for how could she be otherwise?

She is their favourite too because they consider it an extremely funny book, uproariously funny. First there is the part where Mrs. Tittlemouse drives out the black beetle. "Shuh! Shuh! little dirty feet," says the tidy little mouse. "Shuh! Shuh!" say the children to every beetle and spider and fly. "Shuh! Shuh! little dirty feet," I say when they come in with muddy boots, and that is the funniest of all. They hug me with delight. Tiddly-widdly-widdly Mr. Jackson, too, always amuses them, an amiable buffoon with his wet floppy feet and no teeth, but best of all is the spider she bundles out of the window. There is one picture especially, of the spider sitting with its umbrella and Mrs. Tittlemouse peering at it from her hole. For some reason they can never explain, the children find this almost unbearably funny. "What's funny about it?" I ask. And they try to tell. "Look. Look. She's . . ." But whatever it is they are trying to tell is almost lost in helpless giggles, and they can only point.

It begins long before we reach the picture. Pages back I feel them wriggling closer with delight each side of me on the settee. As we get nearer and nearer, odd preliminary chuckles keep bubbling out. "And one day a little old woman ran up and down in a red spotty cloak. 'Your house is on fire, Mother Ladybird! Fly away home to your children!' "

Then they take a big breath and turn the last page. There she is with her spider, and the children are swept up on a great gale of laughter, rocking backwards and forwards against the cushions, throwing their legs in the air.

And I shall never know what it is, sitting there between them as unamused as Queen Victoria, waiting for them to finish, thinking I must fetch some more coal for the fire, and that the inglenook needs painting.

Now that the wet is over, the threshing-machine has arrived on the farm, with its troupe of servants to feed and tend it. He must thresh out some seed-corn, the Farmer says, ready for when the land is dry enough for drilling, and some beans for the animals, to last until the pasture is fit for grazing.

So tonight the threshing-machine stands in the rickyard, mysteriously draped with tarpaulins like an unpresented statue, and the children creep between the wheels to look at what they call the underneath workings. Bright red it is, for all farming machinery is for some reason painted in bright disarming colours, scarlet and sky blue, emerald green and yellow, like children's toys.

Tomorrow it will roar all day, a friendly dragon digesting the sheaves into their simpler parts, grain, chaff, straw, and weed-seeds. And the Farmer tries in vain to tell me how it works, for I do not like machines. He would do better to explain it to the children, since any child nowadays seems to understand more about machinery than any adult—even John, who turns my flute-edged baking-tins against each other like cog-wheels. "Clog-wheels," he calls them, "because they clog each other," he says, "and don't slide off, and when I turn one, it turns all the row."

For a week or more the machine will devour the ricks, and the muddy yard will disappear under soft piles of chaff and silky-looking straw, an unreal pale-gold world in this grey Winter. For it is greyer than ever now the flood has gone, and last night I dreamt of the hot sun of Arles in Provence, only to wake sadly in this wilderness of wet fields.

Arles is not at all as Van Gogh painted it. It is very old. Not, for all its Roman theatre and arena, old in its buildings, but in the sense everywhere of a long unbroken tradition. Life here, one feels, has practised its perfection for centuries, but it is ebbing now, with empty houses falling down in the heart of the town, and new people living in new villas out along the river.

One should see it first from Trinquetaille across the Rhône. A great gentle sky, milky blue in Spring and innocent as Douanier Rousseau's naïve heavens. But the river is alive and evil, muddy and sinisterly swift through the flat valley, so active an enemy that to cross the makeshift bridge is to walk in reach of a tiger tied only on a string.

And between the unaging sky and river is the ancient mortal city, crumbling into golden ruins.

The test of good sculpture, they say—it is one of the

reassuringly simple generalizations—is whether one wants to touch. But touch is not a simple sense. First there is stroking, the most obvious contact with shapes, and this I suppose is the "touching" of most sculpture, following the curves with hand as well as eye. But there are subtler variations. Glass is a surface too cool and smooth and flowing for stiff fingers, only the close tongue will do, licking and sucking. It seems a pity that generally one scarcely can. Then there are shapes and textures one needs to crumble between the fingers like pastry: Gothic stone-work and the piled-up temples of southern India, the *Winged Victory* in the Louvre. And the stones of Arles.

Little dark figures scurry across the bridge and vanish into the disintegrating ant-heap. For Arles, inside the walls, has no main streets like paths through woods, and you must find your way from alley to alley, never knowing when you will come on some new tunnel between the gregarious houses.

There are two main squares in the old town, one shady green, with market stalls under tall plane trees, and its two rival hotels set intimately across the friendly space. The other is austerely beautiful. Stone and sun. Nothing else. No trees, no grass, no fountains. In the scattered reflected light of a northern land it might well be monotonous, but here where the clear sunlight revolves the shadows and varies constantly the emphasis of the masses, it becomes a different architectural composition with every hour of the day. And at night the stones are warm to lean against, long after the air is cool and the tiny owls have begun calling from the trees in the boulevard at the end of the street, their eyes gleaming red in the passing car-lamps.

But here at the damp end of Winter the children are

lunching with the threshers, leaning in a row against a haystack out of the wind. They have taken a billycan of milk, and sandwiches wrapped in newspaper since I have no red handkerchief. And they hand their sandwiches round to the workmen, pressing them to take one, hoping for chunks of bread and cheese in exchange. "He holds the bread on his tummy," John says, "and he cuts it with a sharp knife. And never cuts himself at all. Not once." And the cheerful, dusty men still shout across at each other in the quiet, as they have shouted all morning against the roaring, rattling, thumping machine.

From this house there is one very particular pleasure of threshing—that by some arrangement of the barns and orchard, the noise and shouting comes, not from the rick-yard where it is going on, but as an echo on the other side of the house. And I go so often to the door away from the threshers, to listen to the echo and tell whether the children are still with the men, that in the end I almost think I see a team of ghosts spectrally threshing in the deserted barley-field, as thin and pale as the Ancient Mariner's crew of phantoms.

I do try always not to fuss the children, believing the fuss does more harm than the accidents, but sometimes they go too far. I think it does them good to tumble in the stream. I do not mind when they fall out of trees. Even when they climb up the workman's ladder on to the roof, I look very hard the other way and tell myself that they have never so much as fallen downstairs. *But they must not climb on top of the threshing-machine when it is going.*

THE threshing is over now, and the red machine has gone slowly down the drive and away, taking its court of dusty followers. And we have spent the Winter afternoon, the children and I, in the deserted rick-yard. Even February's pale sun shines with a watery gold among the remaining hayricks, arranged snugly in rows like cottages in a dolls'-house village.

The children tumble in the loose straw, and burrow in the chaff of last week's threshing, while I lie half asleep and recover from wash-day in a part-used haystack, happy in its cleanness, and faint sweet smell, and the pathetic stiff grasses and brown clover flowers like a fossil Summer. From the top of my haystack the familiar countryside is changed because I am ten feet higher. The willows along the stream are silhouetted against green grass instead of sky, I can see the pattern of fields which is hidden by hedges at ground level.

The country on fine Winter days is more beautiful than at any other time. The views have a remote fairy-tale quality, and the bare trees are as fragile as lace. It seems too delicate a composition to be left out in the bad weather. Perhaps that is what Dylan Thomas felt too: "Here in this ornamental Winter, Down pelts the naked weather."

Then the feeling one has of certain bits of country, that this place has a secret life of its own, is a world complete in itself like the world of a picture, this is even more intense in the still withdrawal of Winter.

For some places have a quite inexplicable significance for us, some valley perhaps, or clearing in a wood, or sometimes only a bend in the road, or some angle of the hedges round a field. "Here," one used to feel, "is where it will happen. Round the next corner, beyond the first trees, here I shall find it." But what it was I hoped to find I never knew. As a child I would watch for hours from some leafy hiding-place, wait for the secret which would change my whole life. But I never saw anything at all, only unsuspecting birds searching for grubs in the fallen leaves, and once a weasel like a yellow snake.

At twenty, though one no longer hid and watched, being too self-conscious even alone in one's own company, there was still a strange excitement in certain places, a feeling that this was where important things would happen, that just this arrangement of fields and trees and hills was somehow significant. And I felt then, as I always shall, that we must sit still in the same place for a long time, if anything that matters is to happen to us.

I never knew what it was I expected, and now I never shall know, realizing at last that there are no unpredictable surprises round the corner, no difference of *kind* in one's life, only an enriching and rearranging of the material one has already. It is like the man in the story who wandered round the world seeking his true love, and when he came back disappointed, found that she lived next door and he had known her all his life.

These still Winter afternoons we are visited by flocks of thousands of starlings gathered on the farm. They never come in the morning, accepting the morning, it seems, as a serious working-time, but arrive on fine afternoons, generally on Sundays, as if they too recognized Sunday as traditional time off. They are about for hours, wheeling and turning, chattering and crooning, settling like locusts on every ridge of the house. And when we drive them off for the mess they make, they fly up all at once with a swish of wings, to settle in murmurous complaining in the elms by the stream, thick as Winter leaves. From time to time their chatter swells to an excited climax, then sudden silence, and away they go in swirling clouds to settle in the front meadow, walking like purposeful lice in the short grazed grass.

Every evening towards dusk they fly over us again, not in the great Sunday-afternoon gatherings so absurdly like an excited school-party, but in small groups and singly, flying straight now and no nonsense, heading due west and easier to set a course by than the sliding stars, flying to roost in the willow beds by the river where they live. For it is only at nesting-time that they annoy us under the eaves.

And now along the stream the orange bark of the willows has begun to brighten as the sap rises with the approaching Spring, so that more than ever the twigs look like airy cages painted on to the finished background of the landscape, like the trees in Quattrocento paintings.

But bother the light on the hills, and the willows can flame into fire for all I care. I am tired of the Winter, and tired of the country. Tomorrow I shall put on my town hat and go to London.

So the children have spent the day with an old friend in the village. She keeps rabbits and chickens at her cottage door, there is a pond at the end of her garden, five small children live over the hedge, her son has a ferret in a cage and takes his bicycle to pieces most evenings on the kitchen floor. And as the final perfection in such a world of delights, her husband works on the romantic railway. Who could imagine a more promising day?

And so the children seem to think. They got up as soon as they woke, dressed themselves in their Wellington boots, gobbled breakfast, and from half past seven onwards sat on the top bar of the farm gate to watch for her coming on her bicycle down the drive.

"You look funny," said John, seeing me in my London hat. "You look funny. You look smart."

For I have been to London, through the chalk hills and past Shardeloes, through the indistinguishable suburbs and the wheeling seagulls to London, so dear and so doomed. Such a lovely fragile city it seems now in its sorrow and dignity. Crumbling stone and hollow shells of brick, no more solid against the next bombing than the children's sandpies. The willowherb is bright on the Summer hills, but brighter on the ruins of the city. Fireweed they call it, for it follows destruction.

Shardeloes is an early eighteenth-century house built by Stiff Leadbetter and later enlarged and decorated by Robert Adam. There it stands, on the usual hillside overlooking a watered valley, a solid pile, ton upon ton of stone, in style severely classical, yet somehow it is an ethereal palace from a fairy-tale. For it is strange how eighteenth-century buildings always have that feel in England. Gothic churches are part of the countryside, Tudor houses grow from the earth they stand on, but classical mansions are always castles from Spain. We are never quite sure they are true, these palaces which seem to float on mist, too delicate to be real.

Yet why should a heavy square portico look more fragile than a slender Gothic spire? Perhaps because, designed for the sun, these classical orders take on, in so unsuitable a climate, the delicacy of exotics. Perhaps because, as someone said, we think of them as the line engravings which generally depict them, and not as solid masses. Perhaps because they belong to the Latin conception of man's dignity, and so are as remote and strange for us as Cathay.

Shardeloes looks its loveliest from the morning train, with the shadows of its beeches long across the lawns. For it faces north, as the eighteenth-century houses so often do—Blenheim and West Wycombe. Did they prefer the cool northern light, I wonder, or did they simply take over quite uncritically the shady Italian style, as the Elizabethans took over the classical authors, quoting Pliny for the English weather?

Often I miss the view of the house, looking out of the opposite window for a deep valley in the chalk called Little Switzerland, where the fir trees, seen from above, are as neat and composed as cats sitting by the fire in the circle of their tails. And coming home at night I am too weary to bother about either houses or trees, and can only compose my face for the public carriage before I fall asleep in my corner, as worn out as the country mouse after his day in the city.

Today, even if I have only found half the socks and pans and books and curtains I went for, I have laid a ghost which has troubled me for months. For whenever I go to London lately, I can scarcely think what I am doing because of the tum-te-tum tune of Beethoven's Turkish March from *The Ruins of Athens* going on in my head. But today I stood still as soon as it started, and tracked it down to its beginning. It is the bomb-sites.

They really do not look much like the Acropolis, these squalid brick-heaps, and it is humiliating to find that one's unconscious mind has so little discrimination, but there it is. I pass one of the many derelict buildings, "*The Ruins of Athens,*" I must say to myself without knowing, and at once my head is ringing with the tiresome, insistent march, so that I walk in step, go striding past the shops I meant to go into. Even now the tune still starts up from time to time when I pass outsize ruins like John Lewis, but in a fitful, shamefaced way, like someone caught playing a trick.

But London for the day is too exhausting, hurrying to get through a long list of shopping, with nowhere in the noise and crowds to sit down and recover. It is a relief to climb out of the stale carriage into the chilly country evening and the smell of the station's absurd kerosene lamps. And walking back to the farm through the quiet dark is a gradual return to the different world of our life in the country, the life we have made for ourselves in the shelter of the old house. From the station to the church the road belongs to the outside world, but the lane from there is ours. Down to the stream, where the shadow of the great ash tree branching in the moonlight is like the roads and tracks of some strange country. Through the field gate and along the drive, through the farm gate and across the yard, through the orchard gate and over the stream, past the apple trees and over the moat to the garden gate. Then at last the house itself, the inmost sanctuary.

The night is very still, only a soft, comfortable lowing from a cow in the yard, and a dog barking a long way off. For in the country at night there is always a dog barking a long way off. Dimly through the windows there is a light burning in the hall like a ship at sea, the bricks are silver in the moonlight, and the great roof of the house takes on strange shadows, with somewhere beneath its hilly landscape the sleeping children.

PART TWO

SPRING

THE SPRING HAS COME SUDDENLY AS IT does at the end of February, on some still evening after rain with the thrushes singing late. But this year triumphant in the morning.

For today we woke up unexpecting to radiant sun and warm winds, and set open all the windows on to the summery air. All day I have walked in and out of the house, only for the pleasure of being surprised each time at the mildness. By the end of Winter we are so used to the cold that, without knowing, we contract and wrap ourselves in on the doorstep. So that expanding in this languorous air of the first warm day, we feel that something has gone, some restraint or stimulus, the astringency of the cold. Today gusts of warm air wander through the house. Cold winds blow in a hard, steady stream, but warm ones in loose puffs—*bouffant* would be the exactly right word if it did not mean something else.

It is too soon yet for leaves or flowers or even buds.

SPRING

The grass is dry and dead still after the frost. The garden is littered with withered odds and ends of twigs and dead leaves and straw blown in from the cow-yard, and the countryside looks more hopeless and dishevelled than at any other season. For the land in very early Spring is an untidy dereliction, like a house we have lived in all Winter and only notice with the first sunshine how badly it needs spring-cleaning. Spring today is only in the mercurial sky, which like the sea is always renewed, never aging, only in the soft, flooding sunlight healing the wounds of Winter's battering.

The children have spent the day in the stream, sailing sticks and cotton-reels for boats. I found them at lunch-time wet to their waists and so covered with mud that only their eyes shone out bright like Negro minstrels'. I had told them, they said, that when it was Summer again they could play in the stream. And it must be Summer because it wasn't cold. But still it wasn't warm enough to take off all their clothes like last year's Summer. So they'd "got a bit wet," they said, "but it doesn't matter."

For nothing matters today, this happiest landmark of the country year. The cold will come back, of course. There may be weeks still of frost and cutting winds to snub the first impulsive buds, but after today we can believe in the Spring again, as we had almost ceased to believe through the long Winter. The cold now will be only an impatient interlude in our confidence of Summer, "the farwel frosts of March," as Evelyn calls them.

There are only two occasions when I know for certain, without fear of disappointment, that I shall be happy. One of them is lying in the sun this first warm day of the year, and the other is coming round after an operation.

Under the anæsthetic we drown in so deep a pool of

unconsciousness that we lose all sense of the world going on without us, as we almost never lose it in sleep. After the anæsthetic we come back mentally to where we sank, and the operation is just beginning. Then someone says: "It's all over," and there is a moment of complete happiness. We have no responsibilities to sober us, no worries beyond ourselves, we are simply an ill person getting well again, and irresponsibly happy. Afterwards we shall be sick, uncomfortable, bored, anxious, impatient, but just now we are still deliciously half asleep, our life does not exist beyond the close circle of the bedside lamp, and our small world is flooded with warm content.

All the same, it does perhaps seem a somewhat excessive preparation for a few seconds' pleasure. It is simpler to sit against the south wall of the house and close one's eyes against the warm dazzle, hoping to get brown with the sun. I never hear people talk about the black-coated worker without thinking of him also as the pale-faced worker. For in England, if you are brown, you are either poor and work out of doors, or rich and can take the fine weather off to lie in the sun. The black-coated worker, being neither rich nor poor, is pale except for the week after his Summer holiday.

And our pale skin is ugly in the sunshine, like the underneath of a fish, like plants grown in cellars. So Spring is full of troubles, and not only the spring-cleaning. Suddenly these brilliant days, and how shall we welcome them, pale and shabby after the Winter? The children do well enough with their new gloss hair and peachy skins, but not us with our faces a year tireder every time. We long to be as new-made and radiant as a daffodil, not from vanity, but from the need to make a suitable gesture to the immaculate season. "My love is most immaculate, white and red." I never see carnations in a flower shop, those most rigidly perfect of flowers, without saying it to myself: "Most immaculate, white and red." Well we are not, not grown-ups at the end of Winter.

THE country has settled back to February weather after the week-end Spring, as a sleeper sinks back luxuriously to sleep, waking too early in the morning. A relief it is, faced with the yearly upheaval of the Spring, to be granted a little longer of Winter respite, *"L'hiver saison de l'art serein, l'hiver lucide."*

For Spring, take what precautions we may, is really too upsetting, as painful always as the tingling in a numbed limb as it comes back to life. But perhaps it will be one of the compensations of middle-age to come through February untroubled. For February is the cruellest month, not April, whatever Mr. Eliot may say. The full reality of Spring, the sweet Spring, the year's pleasant king, leaves no time for introspection, for anything but delight. But Mr. Eliot and I do not agree about the Spring at all. "Mixing memory and desire," he says, but for me there are no memories in the Spring. It brings either a new love for the new Summer, or an impersonal delight in the season for its own sake. Even the despairs of Spring are impersonal—that flowers wither in a day, and youth is soon gone, Lyly's sad advice to "waste not the pleasant time of thy youth, than which there is nothing sweeter, nothing swifter." It is the first February vision of Spring which brings the restless discontent, a need for one's own wintry life to blossom into colour and adventure, as soon the orchard will. It was surely in February that Bacon felt "a man would die, though he were neither valiant nor miserable, only upon a weariness to do the same thing so oft, over and over." But we neither die nor blossom, only spring-clean the shabby house.

SPRING

The discontent passes with the real flowering, but Spring is an impossible season and tiresome in all its stages. Pagan, uncivilized, overwhelming, like going over the Niagara Falls helpless in a barrel. The end of Spring, as it floods into Summer, brings a different, half-delicious trouble, as languid and exotic as the early French romances, Aucassin and Nicolette, and Provence in April. This is Mallarmé's Spring, *"le printemps maladif"*:

> *Je tombe énervé de parfums d'arbres, las,*
> *Et creusant de ma face une fosse à mon rêve,*
> *Mordant la terre chaude où poussent les lilas,*
> *J'attends, en m'abîmant que mon ennui s'élève.*
> *Cependant l'Azur rit sur la haie et l'éveil*
> *De tant d'oiseauz en fleur gazouillant au soleil.*

It has always been my favourite Mallarmé sonnet, perhaps because it is one of the few I can understand, for my French is sadly unequal to the more rarefied atmosphere of things like *"le vierge le vivace et le bel aujourd'hui,"* however often the enchanting first line invites me to try.

If I were shut for years in a dungeon without track of the seasons, I think I should still know when it was Spring. For two things happen. First I find myself saying scraps of poetry which I must have learnt at some time, but had long ago forgotten—whole poems from the *Ring of Words*, a great favourite as a child but never seen since, *Peacock Pie*, Masefield and Housman from my adolescence, odd lines and snatches from goodness knows where. It is only in the Spring that I can recite the whole of Keats's odes and Shelley's *Adonais*, a dozen of Shakespeare's sonnets reasonably accurately, Yeats, and Milton's ode on the Nativity, pages of Traherne and bits of *Piers Plowman*, a whole unlikely collection quite forgotten all the rest of the year. It is as if my mind were a muddy pool stirred up by the Spring, and all kinds of drowned fragments come floating to the top like the bits in boiling soup.

Only sometimes can I track down the chance association which has caught up the submerged scrap like a hooked fish, and enjoy the same satisfaction as detective-story readers must, following the clues:

> *We look before and after,*
> *And pine for what is not;*
> *Our sincerest laughter*
> *With some pain is fraught;*
> *Our sweetest songs are those that tell of*
> *saddest thought.*

And so on through Shelley and his skylark all today long, each time I went down the hall. And all day I have groped for the clue until at last I found it—a heap of newspapers waiting in the dairy to light the fires, and there on top was an advertisement for "Someone's Soap Washes Whiter," with grey and white pictures headed Before and After. So I turned over the newspaper face downwards, and have been untroubled since by the poet's airy, insubstantial skylark, a blithe spirit of a bird, which surely never laid a real egg, or looked for earthly worms.

It is tiresome when I am busy, this reciting in the middle of the morning, but the other symptom of Spring is even more bewildering. For without warning or reason I am suddenly possessed by intense vivid memories of places I have seen. Though memory is the wrong word, for during the time that the vision lasts I am actually in the very place itself, hear its noises, smell its smells, feel the wind hot or cold. It is a scene re-created, and infinitely more vivid than the place I am in, although it was never consciously remembered at all until that moment. And they seem quite chance irrelevant places, the corner of a field, a path through a wood seen once long ago, the Yorkshire cliffs of childish holidays.

Without any warning I am transported for that fleeting fraction of time. Between one word and the next I have watched the shadows of the clouds on Great Whernside, between left foot and right gazed at the flat sea across marshes of sea lavender, and heard the redshanks call.

But we are back in Winter again, like getting back into a bath when we had jumped out to answer the telephone.

> *The wireless threatens frost,*
> *And how shall we recapture,*
> *Huddled against this inexpansive season*
> *The large caresses of warmer Springs?*

The trouble with reading W. H. Auden is that, even more than with most writers, everything comes out afterwards in a poor sort of imitation. Well, I shall go back to Bacon, who is inimitable, having no mannerisms, but a gem-like perfection. "Men fear death, as children fear to go in the dark." No sideways glances at the sickroom or grieving friends, no nodding plumes or heavy lilies, but simply and superbly—men fear death. And again: "The joys of parents are secret, and so are their griefs and fears: they cannot utter the one, nor they will not utter the other. Children sweeten labours, but they make misfortunes more bitter: they increase the cares of life, but they mitigate the remembrance of death." It is the influence of the classics at its magnificent best, the ideal discipline, one feels, for an English writer.

Still it is not Bacon I meant to read these last weeks before the Spring, but the books the library has belatedly sent me. For our local library has a bewildering habit of suddenly producing books one wanted months before and had quite forgotten. So that now I have Oscar Wilde, asked for as the first book of the Autumn, for he would be amusing, I thought, after the unsophistication of late Summer, but artificial and out of context now on this edge of Spring.

Reading the brilliant repartee of the first trial, I cannot help feeling what a pity it was for everyone that he could not make do with the opposite sex, when no one would have persecuted him for his vagaries. But it was really no use from the start. "Cold mutton," he said, when they suggested young women. And indeed the proper sense of delicious sin is hard to come by in love-affairs as in everything else. Or why should the intelligent and educated men of the Hell-Fire Club go to the fantastic trouble of building a church on the height of West Wycombe Hill, and climbing up into the ball on top, simply to feel wicked while they sat huddled together on hard benches drinking the wine they had brought with them? They could not even straighten up their heads as they sat, for I have climbed in and tried.

Oscar Wilde too needed to feel he was embracing some mysterious evil. "Like feasting with panthers," he said of his young men, "the danger was half the excitement." And it is easy to understand how loving women and begetting children might seem humdrum and over-obvious, the virtuous duty expected by society and arranged for by nature.

Yet Baudelaire managed to feel for women all that Wilde felt for his young men. His wantons are convincingly and deliciously evil. There is especially the one (I forget her name, or even whether she had one) who wears only her jewels gleaming against her skin in the firelight. And there is Dorothée, who is still my favourite despite her doll-like name, for I always feel she was cleaner than the rest. Massaged with fragrant oils, he says, and there she lies among the cushions, *"tranquille et toujours préparée,"* fanning her breasts languidly among the flowers and weeping fountains.

What a pity that Oscar Wilde could not manage it too, this feeling of danger and evil and excitement in loving women, so that he need not have broken himself against public opinion, but lived to become the delightfully witty and eccentric old man he would surely have been.

The details brought forward in the trials are sordid enough, but then so all prostitution is sordid when looked at in cold blood; and if male prostitution is evidence against homosexuality, female prostitution is equally evidence against ordinary marriage. Nor is it his life by which we must judge Oscar Wilde, and certainly not by his unfortunate attempts at seriousness, but by his brilliant witty comedies.

For man can exist on three different planes, as an animal, as a human being, and as an artist. And when we have decided where he belongs, his existence in the other categories becomes unimportant. Animals must be judged as animals (prize-fighters and beauty queens), humans for the life they live, artists for their work. We do not judge a beauty by whether she can write poems, or a poet by his measurement in inches. But it is just as irrelevant to judge either of them as human beings. Reasonably we should no more expect the beauty to be kind to her old mother, than the kind daughter to be beautiful. Yet we do. We should not expect the poet to be a good father, any more than the good father to be a poet. What they do, or even what happens to them on planes outside their own, is of no importance except as it influences their work, and that, for all the biographers and psychologists may make out, is very little. For both work and behaviour are the product of some inner essence which lives by its own laws. Perhaps even the things which happen to us only happen because we are that sort of person. Some people seem to attract events to themselves like a magnet. So that even our fate perhaps is the creation of our own personality, as it is in Greek tragedy.

The creative artist is only incidentally a human being. His human status is as irrelevant for him as the animal status is for us: essential but unimportant, like one's digestion. He may be an indifferent father, a bad husband, an execrable neighbour, but this is not the sphere in which he exists; except incidentally, as the rest of us exist incidentally as food-eating animals. He is no more to be condemned for behaving unsuitably than we are for eating unsuitably. His laws are the laws of creative art, as incomprehensible to us as the Ten Commandments to a monkey, but for him the only relevant authority.

Of course it is more convenient for everyone if he can manage to pay his debts and not have too many illegitimate children, not cut off his ears or be always giving gold cigarette-cases to valets. But it is of no importance: no more than gossip about the famous. It is the world the artist creates which is vital, not the world he happens to live in. The lives which matter are those of people who use living as their medium of expression, the saints and heroes and villains, and if an artist can express himself in one medium, he is unlikely to do so in another. Shakespeare's mercifully anonymous life is no more likely to be significant than a bullfighter's unwritten prose.

But all creative art, the fashionable psychologists tell us, is sublimated sex. Well, we need not believe it, for there are other fashions, but never mind. And all good roses, the gardener says, need dung. Very well. But it is the *roses* we are interested in. We need not, unless we are gardeners, be bothered with the soil, nor, unless we are psychologists, with Baudelaire's case-history. For neither the dung nor the neurosis explains the work of art. They are only accidents which stimulate the rose tree or the potential artist. They do not explain why the tree bears roses or the man writes poems. They are the fuel which works the machine, but they do not explain how one driver finds his way to El Dorado, while the rest go round in circles or crash into brick walls. It is not the water in the river which interests us, but the valley it makes for itself.

Oscar Wilde and reproductions of El Greco's paintings—these are my Autumn library books so unsuitable for the Spring. No one has ever painted women as passionately as El Greco painted men, and these smouldering intensities are not for the sunny out-of-door season. If Michel Angelo's women are all men, equally El Greco's men are all women. Yet they are neither one nor the other, these strange androgynous figures, curiously sexless for all their intensity of flesh. Their beautifully distorted bodies sway like flames in the force of their passion, for they are neither men nor women, but the embodiment of desire.

The writer who comes closest to El Greco is Gerard Manley Hopkins. We seem to feel through his difficult poetry (surely difficult for him writing as much as for us reading) the same passionate nature deflected—by conscience perhaps, or some personal idealism, but deflected certainly—into religion. "To what serves mortal beauty?" Hopkins asks. "Dangerous; does set dancing blood." So he turns to Christ, "as a stallion stalwart," he says, "very-violet-sweet," and he might be describing El Greco's lovely languishing figures on the cross. And because we have no longer any taste for physical passion mixed up with religion, we are offended. But our distaste is no more than a matter of fashion, and the greatest seventeenth-century religious verse is as rapturous as any love poetry.

I wonder if Hopkins was thinking of El Greco's paintings when he described Harry Ploughman, or whether it was that they both had the same strange vision of human forms, for Hopkins is an intensely visual poet. "The rack of ribs; the scooped flank; lang rope-over thigh; knee nave; and barrelled shank"—it describes exactly a dozen of El Greco's straining figures.

He leans to it, Harry bends, look. Back, elbow, and
liquid waist
In him, all quail to the wallowing o' the plough: 's cheek
crimsons; curls
Wag or crossbridle, in a wind lifted, windlaced—
See his wind-lilylocks-laced.

Nor is it only El Greco's figures which Hopkins describes, but his menacing backgrounds of stormy chaos, so suggestive of the sea although he never paints it. These backgrounds are the setting for the wreck of the *Deutschland* when "frightful a nightfall folded rueful a day."

For the infinite air is unkind,
And the sea flint-flake, black-backed in the regular blow,
Sitting Eastnortheast, in cursed quarter, the wind;
Wiry and white-fiery and whirlwind-swivellèd snow
Spins to the widow-making unchilding unfathering deeps.

Sometimes, indeed, as in *Saint Martin and the Beggar,*

the sky is peaceful, but still the clouds have a curiously solid look, like sacks, says Hopkins:

Up above, what wind-walks! what lovely behaviour
Of silk-sack clouds!

This for me is one of El Greco's most perfect single pictures—so many of the big ones I can only take in by dividing them into separate pieces. There is often, for instance, a tiny, quite magical picture in one corner, like the centurions and the moonlit lake beyond, at the right of the National Gallery *Christ in the Garden*, where the disciples too are curled up asleep in their own close composition, like an X-ray of triplets in the womb. Or again, the figure with a pitcher on her head on the right of the *Christ in the Temple*.

But *Saint Martin and the Beggar* is a complete whole. The young beggar's naked beautiful body flows in passionate yearning towards the boy on the horse. And he hesitates, the dreaming boy on the dreaming white horse, stirred but only half awakened, sheltered in his armour. The curly-haired youth (and how often El Greco loved to paint those clustering ginger curls) rode out into the blue morning, his head cloudy with romantic visions, and he has found instead this consuming human passion. He still hesitates, but already their hands are consciously close, it is the focus of the design, and in a moment—beyond the tranced suspended moment of the picture—their hands will touch and it will happen.

How young men of his time must have dreamed of seeking out such a painter. But surely they would only have found disappointment, for one who could so vividly express himself in paint could have no need of any more fleeting reality.

· · ·

SPRING

"Let's go for a walk," said John. "Let's go to the rail-way bridge," he said, in the tone of pleased surprise with which people announce new ideas. As if going to the rail-way bridge were not our standard family walk, where we go so often that even the birds along the hedges recognize us as harmless facts of nature, like the farmcarts and the tractor, not bothering to fly up from their nests as we pass, unless we shoo them off to see if the eggs are hatching. Half a mile there, just over half a mile back, for we go round by the far ploughing, it is exactly the right distance for the children's walking powers. And since it is over the fields it does not matter how long they loiter picking cowslips and chimney-sweep grasses in short-stalked bunches, for I can lie by the stream under the hum of bees in the willow-catkins, and watch the lap-wings soar and dive and call despairingly to keep us from their nests on the ploughing.

The railway bridge is a modest arch under the single-track line, scarcely high enough for the piled Summer hay-carts to push under, brushing the top. But it has an echo which fascinates the children. "Woh," they say, never anything else. "Woh-woh-woh." And one of them goes through to the other side to make sure it is really an echo which answers and not the Farmer come to tease them.

Then through the arch there is the boat pool, a deep hollow in the stream, which is dammed up here for some reason, so that the Winter's driftwood collects in slowly turning rafts, like seaweed in the Sargasso Sea. The children cling to my hand, and lean over to fish out likely-looking logs, and carry them back home in triumph to make new boats. A long nail knocked in the middle, a cotton-reel fitted on to it for funnel, and what could be a more convincing steamer? Sometimes when I have done extra sewing, their ships can have three funnels, but then, by the tiresome laws of gravity and the weight of nails, they tend to float upside down, and must be weighted with stones tied underneath.

The Farmer often comes with us to the bridge, to count the calves on the far grazing and make sure that none are in trouble, and the children, as well as me, are delighted with his company, because he hooks them pieces of wood we cannot reach ourselves. One day, stretching out for a log which floated tantalizingly in the middle, his watch slipped out of his pocket and disappeared in the brown water. So in the afternoon we came back with a magnet on a string, and took it in turns to balance on planks over the dark pool and fish unavailingly for watches.

THE Winter is retreating slowly before the longer sunlight, and the landscape now has the clear rain-washed quality of early Spring, a delicate austerity, as if the urgent, indiscriminate growth of new life were controlled by our chill northern airs, refined to an elegant perfection.

For days now the sun shines and shines, and I am ashamed of my animal high spirits. All today I have been so absurdly happy that I feel I shall float up to the ceiling like a gas-filled balloon, or burst, or turn inside out, or grow four arms like Siva, some expressive and generous expression. I run round the orchard scattering the silly sheep, and pretend I am amusing the children, which I am, hugely. I teach them to stand on their hands on the lawn, and they laugh because I look so tall upside down. I wake in the mornings happy for no reason, as one does wake sad or happy and only afterwards remembers why. But now there is no reason to remember, only that the

Summer is before us, and everything is still to come.

And I have done nothing with my happiness, nothing but clean the house, simply because it is Wednesday, and Wednesday is house-cleaning day, however much today transcends the ordinary Wednesdays. I am so rich that it does not matter that I use golden guineas to work the penny slot-machine.

Still I wish I could dilute this wild exhilaration into a steady background of content. I would like my happiness now to sit in the sun under the dove-cot wall like Juliet's nurse, not this brilliant light of excitement to dazzle my eyes against all else, as it does when we are very young. And I thought, if I could think at all for the laughing, that happiness makes us older, less romantic, less in need of dreams. Discontent, not happiness, is the food of youth and poetry.

In the orchard at the back of the house is an enormous old pear tree, so high that we can see it over the roof from the other side. And every year since we came I have stood under it when it is in blossom and wondered what Hopkins meant when he called it "the glassy pear-tree." This Spring, for the first time, I see. It is partly the texture, the shiny leaves and thin, half-transparent petals, but the colour too, the unemphatic green, the white blossom with no trace of pink. It is like Sabrina's wave, glassy cool translucent, but not so good a poem as Milton's. For Sabrina with her curiously overwrought beauty is one of the very few superlatives, like "Mistress Mine," and "Full Fathom Five," and "Fear No More the Heat o' the Sun" —perfections which hurt to hear, even the twentieth time over. Some of the mediæval lyrics belong here too, "When the turf is thy tower," or "The fish in the flood," or "Where is Paris and Heleyn"—melancholy fragments, for in English all the lyrics one best remembers are sad, from Auden's "Weep no more" right back to the first disconsolate minstrel's tale of past woes, with the unhappy refrain of "That passed over, so may this." "Then stretch our bones in a still gloomy valley," someone sings in a Beaumont and Fletcher play, "Nothing's so dainty-sweet as lovely melancholy." And in England this elegiac mood, a detached, almost formal sadness, seems to suit us best. Perhaps it is because of our melancholy and lovely weather.

Of all forms of poetry the lyric must be the most exacting, if only because there are so few perfect ones. For a lyric must be as perfect and unflawed as a crystal. In so light a form there is nothing to outweigh the smallest error. The slightest fault mars all, of taste or emotion or expression. Wordsworth will not do, he is too earnest. Indeed he is always too earnest; but at his very best, as in *The Ode* or parts of *The Prelude*, he has so much else to offer that we put up with it. And Housman at the other extreme, will not do either—sentimental, theatrical, and far too loosely wordy for all his fine single lines.

> *By brooks too broad for leaping*
> *The lightfoot boys are laid;*
> *The rose-lipt girls are sleeping*
> *In fields where roses fade.*

It might almost be a wicked parody, so irresistibly does it remind us of the dressed-up musical-comedy chorus sadly sentimentalizing. "Many a rose-lipt maiden. And many a lightfoot lad," and then the real ones, the "Golden lads and girls." It is the simplest gold beside the fussy tinsel. Endlessly evocative, as light as a sigh, and as tender:

> *Golden lads and girls all must,*
> *As chimney-sweepers come to dust.*

But hostile criticism is an unpleasant self-indulgence, and if no one is to write because they cannot write like Shakespeare, what shall we all have left to read?

THE children have decorated the kitchen windowsill for the Spring with jam jars of frog spawn and bursting sticky buds. Everything about a horse-chestnut tree, from these huge buds to the great yellow fallen leaves, is on too large a scale, coarse and ungainly. The people of Brobdingnag with their rough, pitted skins must have looked just so to the disgusted Gulliver. But then Swift was so easily disgusted, even that we eat salt with our food, though I could never see why.

Yet horse-chestnuts do well enough massed at a distance, sheer cliffs of solid green with white flowers in May like settled sea-birds. Flowers which, looked at closely, have the same exotic rankness as magnolias. Of all the English trees this most belongs to the jungle. The plants which thrust through the pavements and split the frescoed walls in the Khmer temples of Indo-China must grow with this same cruel exuberance. Even the heavy branches drooping to the ground can root and grow where they touch, a somehow obscene propagation. It is fitting that the horse-chestnut should have been brought to England by the Elizabethans, themselves so exuberant and fantastic.

But for John, sticky buds and tadpoles mean that his birthday is near.

JOHN: "I'm leaning fourward, and tomorrow will be a birthday and I shall *be* four. And then I'll be leaning five-ward. Only Peter's leaning fiveward *now,* and I can't catch up."

Well, he was four last week, but it was no suitable

week for birthdays, so I ignored it, thankful that they cannot yet read calendars. For I announce birthdays when I find it convenient, on sunny days for picnics, or when there has been time to make a birthday cake. A "candle-cake" they call it, caring not at all for the cake under the candles, but only for the candles themselves, which must be lit and blown out a dozen times until they are no more than melting stumps.

Any day now will do for a birthday, for it is high Spring, and the whole countryside is prodigally *en fête*, with miles and miles of blossom and catkins and singing birds. How lucky for us that this serious business of producing seeds and laying eggs should take on so gay and frivolous an air. The old house is absurdly, extravagantly lovely, bowered in pink-confetti apple blossom, with cuckoos like nursery clocks in every tree.

For the townsman, of course, the country is always on holiday. The sun shines continually, the birds sing without stopping, the roses bloom round the door all the year, even on Christmas cards. Corn grows of itself, hens lay speckled eggs for the picking-up, and hay-making, that dreaded crisis of the farming year, is a holiday frolic in the sun.

It is the same when the country goes to the town. For there people wear their best clothes all the time, they walk in the streets and shops during the working-day, they eat luxuriously in restaurants, and sit, even in mid-morning, in deck-chairs in the parks.

Living out here, every Spring there is this same astonishment at the green. For all the rest of the year green is a background colour, as brown is, as grey is in towns. But not in Spring. For this first rush of new green is a colour in its own right, a vivid positive colour, as transformed and unexpected as the brown of pansies. The opening leaves are flowers, are blossoms which sprout on every hedge, bunches of green petals.

This is what townsmen mean by Spring, this high festival which bursts on them suddenly from the naked Winter. Yet living in the country, it does not come suddenly at all, it is only the final crescendo of a long-rising excitement. As early as the New Year the bird-calls change, there are shivering lambs soon after Christmas. Under the dead leaves in hedge-bottoms there are urgent shoots of green, dogs'-mercury and arum-lily leaves. And digging up the last parsnips (too sweet they are, and stringy), the turned earth smells differently, is busier with worms.

After a few mild days the Winter wheat stands out an unlikely blue-green in the mottled landscape of fields, the coltsfoot and hazel are in flower before even the earliest buds show on the blackthorn. And long before the first mist of green in the trees, the tracery of twigs thickens with the swelling sap, and looking closely at the Winter buds of beech and sycamore and chestnut, there are thin pale lines where the bud-scales have started to grow.

"When you can cover two daisies with your foot," says the Farmer, "then you need care for no man." He is as happy as we are that the Winter is over and gone, but too optimistic with his daisy standards, for in a mild season they flower all Winter on our weedy lawn.

He is no bard that cannot sing
The pleasures of the flowery Spring.

Not even the bards can always sing, and I am not even a bard. Of course one can describe the pinkish hairy stalk of a primrose, and for everyone else who has gathered primroses, there is the Spring complete. The watery yellow, the faint, fresh smell, the pale, crinkled leaves, even the banks and woods behind and the showery sky—all this is described by implication for anyone else who has looked at a primrose.

Yet it has nothing much to do with the writer's skill. He has only been lucky to stumble on the right evocative detail, as the first nettle-sting in March on the inside of our wrist will plunge us suddenly into deep Summer, the trees dark and heavy, and the roads dusty in the heat. The primrose writer's only talent is in guessing what will be the experience he is most likely to share with his reader. He has made no magic of his own, like "Nothing is so beautiful as Spring," though why that seemingly simple statement is so moving I can never understand. But the primrose-describer is as far from that as the Pre-Raphaelite painters' copied primroses are from Botticelli's created flowers.

This is the week when the orchard is sweet with a faint but all-pervading scent. Like lilacs it is, but more delicate, more elusive. It is strongest on warm, still evenings after rain, bothering me to trace it every Spring as I come back through the orchard with the evening milk. Strongest then, though still too elusive for the quickly tiring nose. This year I have found it at last. It comes from the opening leaves of the poplars by the stream. Their rosy tassels of pink catkins smell not at all, only the young leaves which follow, and only when the air is damp.

WE have been on our birthday picnic at last, piling the old tank of a pram with bottles of milk, and buns in a bag, and old blankets, not because the ground is damp but for protection against last year's stubble, which makes lying in an unploughed field as uncomfortable as a fakir's spiked board. Off we went, lurching through the rick-yard in the Winter cart-ruts, past the sheep-dip, and over the mushroom field to look at the skeleton of the cow that fell into the bomb-hole and died. Much cleaned-up it is now by the Winter appetites of rats and crows and foxes.

There is a certain bend in the stream which the children especially love, a secret and sudden loop hidden under a tunnel of willows and poplars. And here there is always a little ridge of sand dropped by the water as it slows down round the curving bank. After the Winter rains the sand is thick and smooth and clean as gold; it is always one of our first Spring picnics. I lie in the sun, and the children get wet through. What could be simpler or more satisfactory for everyone?

Yet I doubt whether these two children, with all their obvious advantages, will have a childhood as full and exciting as mine was. I doubt whether any middle- or upper-class child has as rich a life as the working-class have when they are happy. When I was young we were quite poor, and because there was a housing shortage even then, we lived in a street of back-to-back houses in a northern industrial town. And, quite untroubled at that early age by the meanness and ugliness, I delighted in the riotous life of the streets, uncontrolled by the disapproval of my parents, who in any case knew very little of what went on.

I ran wild with the gangs of local children in a lawless community of our own. We knocked on doors (it was too poor there for bells) and ran away chased by some furious father close behind us, for since the door opened straight into the only living-room we never had much start. We rolled dust-bin lids down cobbled streets on windy nights, delirious with happiness in the noise and wind. We played Last Across in front of trucks, making a hero of the one who darted closest under the great approaching wheels. We clung for rides to the backs of vans, we built forts on the derelict brickfields and played at enemy gangs. From August to November we collected great hoards of wood for our Guy Fawkes bonfire, running off with boxes, dragging branches of trees for miles through the streets. "Chumping" we called it, and considered it serious work.

Then there were the traditional games, whose rules we all knew and never dreamt of changing. All Winter I played marbles with the boys, for though this was not really a girls' game, I was considered "queer" and did very much as I liked, preferring the more enterprising company of the boys to the way the girls, even at that early age, would talk personalities. The marbles were treasure which I kept in a blue velvet bag, pulling up with a cord like a sponge-bag. There were very different values in marbles, the unit of reckoning being one, which was an ordinary clay taw. There were slightly larger ones made of stone, and these were worth two, as were the plain glass ones like stoppers in old-fashioned lemonade bottles. Then there was the whole aristocracy of glass marbles with coloured stripes inside in delicate whorled patterns, more charming than any Venetian glass has ever been since. These were worth an "ally" for each colour, an ally being three clay marbles. So that a glass marble with blue, green, and yellow stripes was worth nine clay taws, and our commonest quarrels were about the value of these ally-taws, as they were called, whether pink and red counted as separate colours, and if so, why not light and dark blue?

We played all kinds of games with them besides the ordinary shooting to hit your opponent's marble, but most of them I have forgotten. I still remember Holey, a sort of gambling game with winner-take-all, which seemed to me recklessly extravagant. You scraped out the dirt from a corner of the paving-stones until you had a suitable hole. Then the first player fixed the stakes, ten marbles perhaps, which he rolled all at once towards the hole to see how many he could get in. Each player—and any number could join in—followed with their ten, and whoever got most in the hole took the ten marbles from all the other players. So that if you were lucky, for there was very little skill, you could win a hundred in one game and go away dizzy with riches. If ever you came on a circle of small boys squatting engrossed in the middle of the pavement, they were almost certainly playing Holey, and you could ask the stakes and join in, for you always had marbles in your pocket, as the grown-ups always had money.

Cigarette cards, too, was a boys' game. You each threw your card in turn against a wall so that it fell back on the pavement, and if the card you threw fell on top of a card already thrown, they were both yours. But I never played this, for it made the cards dirty.

At Easter, for the seasons were important, we all played whip and top, a game shared equally by the girls. There were slender carrot tops, and fat jumbos, and on their flat heads we chalked a whole range of coloured patterns to watch them change with the spinning. Best of all I liked one of radiating spokes of all colours of the rainbow, which changed mysteriously to grey as the top spun.

The girls' games were much more varied and complicated, as if it must always be the women who keep the traditions alive. There was German Exercises, a highly skilled and involved counting-game played with a ball against a wall, which the boys loved to watch, but would have considered it a loss of their manhood to join in.

Then there was skipping. First of all, two unfortunates to turn the rope were decided on by saying "Eeny-meeny-miny-mo," and whichever of them first said "Firsyender" was the first relieved when someone was "out." There were endless patterns of skipping, running in and out of the steadily turning rope, playing Follow-my-leader, and skipping with steps as complicated as a country dance. There were rhyming games, too:

> *Raspberry, strawberry, gooseberry jam,*
> *Tell me the name of your young man.*

Then you skipped double fast—"peppering" we called it —saying the letters of the alphabet at each jump until you were out, and that was your young man's initial. And there were dozens of nonsense rhymes, mostly forgotten now, alas—rhymes like:

> *"Little brown doctor*
> *How's your wife?"*
> *"Very well thank you,"*
> *"That's all right."*
> *"But she can't eat a bit of fish*
> *Nor a bit of liquorice."*
> *O.U.T. spells out.*

There. Now some learned professor can trace it back to the Druids.

Then there were the two sorts of Hopscotch, both chalked on the pavement and played with a stone. Box Hopscotch was six squares and two "boxes" fitted into a rectangle, and Round Hopscotch looked like a segmented ammonite coiled on the pavement.

Battledore and Shuttlecock (where do the names come from, I wonder?) was a game for Whitsuntide, but with us it was always suspect. To begin with, anyone who had the sixpence or whatever it was to buy the bat and shut-tlecock was regarded, by a sort of inverted snobbery, as "not one of us." Then it was considered such an excessively feminine game that even for girls to play it was going really too far. I loved to see the flying white feathers, and to stroke them smooth again when they were ruffled, but I knew that if I joined in, it would be the end for ever of playing marbles with the boys.

Chop Chalk, I think, was a game we made up ourselves, a girls' game, but why we called it that I never knew, for there was no chalk and no chopping. We filled our pockets with bits of sandstone picked up on the rubble heaps—it is the first time I remember noticing the different textures of stones—and then we ground the bits down on the edge of the pavement with a flat heavy stone which became as close and personal to us as any craftsman's favourite tool. The resultant sand we stored in boxes which we hid, a secret treasure as precious as gold-dust. One Winter, when the steps to our house were covered with ice, my mother spread them with a handful of my sand to stop us slipping. It seemed to me a truly criminal extravagance.

It was not all, of course, of such May-morning innocence. I learnt all kinds of quite unsuitable words, which I no longer remember because I never understood them. I chalked things on walls. I learnt to make a Spanish thumb without in the least knowing what it meant except that it was wicked. I would make it when I passed respectable people in the street, half expecting to be struck dead by lightning, but no one ever took the slightest notice.

If we had a down on anyone, we would chalk up on a wall that they loved some child or other, all in initials: "A. E. loves B. W." Not because they took any notice of each other, but because we knew it would annoy them more than anything else we could think of. For we considered sex very shocking indeed, not because we knew anything about it, but because the grown-ups, who did, quite obviously found it dreadful and would not discuss it. Though I think if we had not been ashamed of seeming childish by not being in the know, we should all have admitted that we found it a great bore. Certainly we were very conscious of being different sexes, but it was only like being different races, there was nothing shocking or mysterious.

In that vigorous community where every child spoke the broadest Yorkshire dialect and had quite dreadfully bowed legs from the ubiquitous rickets, I was known as "the one with straight legs what talks funny." But never to my face, for with my peculiar straight legs I could easily outrun any of them, and I was quite ruthless where I considered my dignity was threatened.

After a time my family moved to a proper house, with a door back and front, and lots of room for everything to be separate. And though there was a garden and a swing, the children did not play in the streets, and for a time life was very dull and very lonely.

I cannot, out here, give John and Peter my hilarious slum background, but I can at least (or what is the use of living on a farm?) answer their questions about the Facts of Life without any mysterious shame. Yet however we may have decided to be frank and simple about it all, our modesty or prudery—it does not matter what we call it, for anyway it wins. The mother part is easy enough, a neat and convenient arrangement it seems, which they accept and approve. But the father is really too embarrassing. Not for them of course. These, they think, are straightforward uncomplicated procedures, like winding up your train to make it go. But despairing of my courage to give simple answers to simple questions, I sent them off in the end to watch the bull, knowledge they at once enlarged for themselves by watching all the other animals about the farm. Their only interest now is whether fathers bite the mothers' necks like the ducks do.

The animals themselves are as matter-of-fact about it all as the children: the ducks irritable, the sparrows fussy, the cows indifferent. Only the cats seem to have any emotion at all—not, indeed, the proper swooning voluptuousness, but a fierce jungly lasciviousness surprising in a mild English garden.

For really the farm-yard carries self-sufficiency too far. I am always a little ashamed of my sex when the cows turn away to graze, and pigeons, ignoring the most passionate demonstrations, are as persistently cruel as the disdainful fair who so slighted and so inspired the seventeenth-century lyrists. But then if we were more responsive, there might be no rainbows on cock-pigeon breast feathers, no love-poems for the anthologies.

All day the courting ducks have been about the orchard, noisy with their sudden excited choruses. But how limiting to be an animal with only a single noise for everything one wanted to say. "Quack Quack," and it may mean: "I'm hungry," or: "I love you," or: "What a lovely morning," or even sometimes: "How bored I am!" though that supposes a perhaps excessively sophisticated duck. Yet cows do look quite convincingly bored, standing for hours unmoving with heads down and tails to the wind, though, for all we self-projecting sentimentalists know, they may be deliciously savouring the last mouthful of hay through a whole cowy morning.

• • •

SPRING

FOR the last week the children have been so exceedingly good, so very law-abiding that I come near to despising them as a pair of little prigs. Certainly they come in covered with oil from riding on the tractor, or wet through from building rafts on the stream. They lose their nerve at the top of trees so that I must climb up and rescue them, they break our few remaining china teacups making sandpies with them—"We're sorry, we didn't know we mustn't have them. You didn't tell us not" (for I was cross, it seems, however unreasonably). "We're sorry, we didn't know they could break."

But still nothing the most carping of parents could logically consider naughty. Yet we went through storms in plenty before we reached this calm weather. For a year, round about the age of two, each of them occupied himself almost exclusively with being naughty. Whenever I had anything to do with them, meals or bathing or bedtime, there were always scenes. Whatever I wanted them to do, they deliberately refused—not, I think, because they disliked me, or even disliked the usual routine, but because they felt themselves for the first time as separate persons, and enjoyed trying out their strength against mine. They gave their whole attention to the struggle, making the most of every smallest advantage, of my tiredness or preoccupation, and though I interfered with them as little as possible, they would make occasions to come and try me out, knowing perfectly well, the young Machiavellis, that I must win every single time if I were to win at all.

In those days they were luckily still small enough to be slapped, so that at least I had some weapon to fight with, since we are curiously powerless against a defiant two-year-old whom we love. He is quite safe, knowing we love him, and that our punishments are mild and predictable, that he has only to give in when he is worsted and it is all over. And smacking they not only expected, but accepted as reasonable, however much fuss they might make to save their face before giving in.

But the last time I slapped John for some obstinate naughtiness, he went off chuckling: "That didn't hurt, that was only playing." Well, if he will not accept it any longer as a token punishment, we shall have to give it up. For if he judges it on its merits, it has never been more than a noisy sort of pat on the back of their hands, scarcely as loud as they clap them together themselves when they are excited. They would never have noticed the smart except for the authority it enforced, but when they were too young to be reasoned with, they recognized it as a simple expression of my stern disapproval, and how comfortably firm that sounds. For we can recognize the power of the law perfectly well without ever being ill-treated by a policeman.

But John does not recognize it any longer, it seems, and we must find something else. How tiresome if I must begin heart-to-heart talks, or the delayed spitefulness of refusing him something he specially wants. And what an emotional disturbance it will create between us, as the slapping never did, I being simply an inevitable stone wall which he bumped his own head against.

Peter I had to give up smacking long ago, for the last time he simply stood tense and white without crying and waited for me to finish. A horrible situation happily ended on my lap in floods of relieving tears. And then and there we made what he calls his Magreement—that I would never smack him any more because he was too old now, but that he must behave like a sensible person and not like an obstinate baby.

Which seems to me a severe strain, and surely it is much easier to be slapped, but he evidently prefers it this way—being a dignified creature, prefers to discipline himself, even though he often dances with frustrated rage in the effort to control himself, to keep his promise because I have kept mine.

How anyone controls very small children without some kind of mild smacking I cannot imagine. It is not only that they have to be dealt with long before they understand words, but even when they do understand what we say, there is nothing to appeal to, no better nature, no feeling for the fitness of things, no sense of justice. Our complicated standards of behaviour are more than their poor heads can make sense of, so quite simply they must do as they are told because we say so.

After all, it is what they will have to do all their lives, and an easier lesson to learn as a baby than later on. What misery and frustration school must be for children who arrive undisciplined, and how frightening to be punished by strangers. With parents they know perfectly well that however much we quarrel with them to enforce the rules, at bottom we are their unswerving friends. Besides, they are stern disciplinarians themselves, as anyone realizes listening to their play. Obedience is one of the things they recognize as necessary, however much they may exercise their self-will in revolt.

I have been reading Florio's Montaigne on the education of children, but really he is no help. "They do very ill that goe about to make it seeme as it (Philosophie) were inaccessible for children to come unto, setting it forth with a wrimpled gastlie and frowning visage. There is nothing more beauteous, nothing more delightful, nothing more gamesome." But I doubt whether John and Peter would find Philosophie gamesome just yet, however much I went about "gently-bidding them to the banquet of letters."

"Silence and modestie," he says again (he can be very prim), "are qualities very convenient to civil conversation." Why, so they are, but at four and five? Still he was writing for a lady whose child was even younger, being not yet born. I only hope she was malicious enough to be amused at such streams of advice from the impractical recluse.

But then he goes on, and this time I echo him from the heart. Ploughing and planting are easy, he says, but tending the growing crop needs much adoe. "So in men, it is no great matter to get them, but being borne, what continual cares, what diligent attendance, what doubts and feares doe daily wait to their parents and tutors before they can be nurtured and brought to any good." His father, he tells us, would have him wakened from sleep by a musical instrument (I wish he had told us what), so as not to rouse him too violently. But I am never awake before the children to practise such delicacies.

Watching John and Peter live their separate lives, I am overwhelmed from time to time that I am in complete control of two human beings. It seems quite incredible that society should consider me reliable enough. For they eat only what I give them, know almost nothing but what I tell them, have no manners or morals or habits of behaviour except what I have taught them. I make their world as I choose, and it astonishes me daily that I should be allowed to do so exactly as I please.

Young children have the gaiety and charm of all young animals, but in any actual child it is an ephemeral quality. Their lovable boneless attitudes, squatting and tumbling, their vivid phrases and quick spontaneous gestures, these in any actual child are as quickly lost as a chicken's fluff. Already these two are changing to an awkward legginess, becoming careful in their talk, outgrowing their first childhood.

The charm of small children is none the less enduring, like the song of the cuckoo, however transient each individual bird. If John looks up at me with his mouth half open and his face brilliant with laughter, a thousand generations of children have looked just so at their delighted elders, and a thousand more to come will look the same. The child himself is infinitely vulnerable. Death in a hundred fashions can destroy him utterly. Even in life, his present self is as transient as Spring flowers, for in a year he will be a new creature, scarcely to be recognized. Yet so long as human beings exist, this exact childish attitude will be handed down unchanged, as if the true reality were the intangible pattern, and no material child.

Charming they may be, but still it is lonely living with children, and at times I long for my fellow creatures, which these are not. For children as young as these are strange animals, and we have no way of understanding each other. They are alien, inhuman beings, less considerate than a dog, less controlled than a horse, less conscious than a cat, their very voices high and shrill as seabirds. They can satisfy none of our emotional needs, yet we must satisfy all of theirs. They must, by their very nature, be completely selfish. They love us, not for what we are in ourselves, but for what we do for them, we who make the very structure and climate of the world they live in. So that bad mothers are loved as dearly as good—more dearly indeed, since the unhappy child clings more desperately, and the stable one takes his protectors confidently for granted.

For they are nervous creatures in a chaotic and unpredictable world whose rules they do not understand. A

new person is a strange animal met in the jungle, and may
be equally friend or foe. Which is why, I suppose, they
accept so readily the small bribes of friendship—a sweet
or a toy—not for the things themselves, but as tokens of
goodwill which they have learnt to consider reliable.
"So-and-so is coming to see us," I say. "Does he like children?" they ask at once, as if any visitor were a dog
which might bite. "Yes," I assure them, and they run off
confidently to say hello. How black and white their
world must be, with no half-tones of indifference.

They seem too to have a disconcerting way of swallowing people whole, of judging by some inner essence
and ignoring the surface smiles and protestations. Or perhaps that is only a romantic fancy of modern psy-
chology, and understanding only the surface, children
are simply more attentive to outward behaviour, to a
tone of voice or a nervous gesture, as dogs are.

It is only rarely that we can reach them with our human standards and emotions. They are driven by their
egoism, in blinkers against the rest of the world, unconscious that any needs exist but their own. Human affec-
tions and moral standards they learn as something strange
and bewildering. They must not do the obvious things
—take what they want, or avoid trouble by lying—because we call it stealing and wicked. But for them our
words mean nothing. Our prohibitions are rocks put in
their path, obstacles they must find a way round, but
something outside themselves, arbitrary and with no intrinsic meaning.

And more almost than affection they need stability. It
does not matter much whether the system is strict or in-
dulgent, since they have no standards to judge by. It
need not even be just, since at this age they have no conception of justice, only of keeping the rules, but they

must understand how the system works, and it must be rock-solid.

Poor Peter—too ill, I thought, to be punished, however naughty—simply went on with the offence in desperate tears.

ME: "Do you want me to smack you?"

PETER: "Yes, I do. You're *supposed* to."

And who would not rather be slapped by the known rules than feel

> *The pillared firmament is rottenness*
> *And earth's base built on stubble?*

I am surprised too, every day, by the bewildering speed at which young children change. They are like a boiling cauldron which will crystallize out in time, but is still, from moment to moment, in seething movement. A year changes the young as much as ten years their parents, as if the grown-up state were a broad plateau which we climb to in youth. The shy, leggy schoolgirls of our first arrival here are plump now and married, and confidently with child. And I have not even altered the way I do my hair.

It seems to me now that the world outside me changes faster than I do myself, yet the children feel they live in a static unchanging universe, so much faster is their own development. As two trains, passing and re-passing each other as they run into London, seem first one, then the other, to be moving or still.

I remember throughout my own adolescence (it is almost the only emotion of any kind which I do remember) an endless sterile boredom. In desperation I longed for any catastrophe, for fire or war or earthquake, anything to break the dreadful spell and make the static world come alive again. Yet to an adult, the uneasy period between the wars must have seemed a long up-heaval.

TODAY at tea we played at Silly Eggs, the children's name for a game which has all the feel of becoming a family tradition. They eat their boiled egg, put the empty shell upside down in the egg-cup, and pass it to me with a most charming smile. "Dear Dardy, here's an egg for your tea. A lovely egg. All for you. You eat it."

ME: "Oh, how very nice. I just wanted an egg. I feel very hungry."

THEM: Giggles.

ME: "What a funny noise" (tapping the egg with a spoon). "It sounds hollow. I expect that means it's a specially nice one."

THEM: More giggles, and much wriggling about on their stools with delighted anticipation.

So I must go tapping and exclaiming until I break through to emptiness, and they both fling themselves back with laughter at my pretended rage.

But the game is not over, for children are more, and not less, amused at jokes they have heard before. I am handed the other egg to do it all over again for my insatiable audience, only glad that I have no more egg-eating children to demand further encores.

It is not only that they know it is teasing, but they know I know too. They even know I know they know, which is one stage of consciousness further than Coventry Patmore's sleeping lady. There is no mystery, no surprise, but, like Greek tragedy, it never fails to work. And quite soon now I can get them to do the play-acting instead of me, and I can sit back and enjoy the spectacle of them mimicking me mimicking someone surprised at an empty egg.

SPRING

What bird sings, yet does so wail?
O, tis the ravished Nightingale.

It is Lyly, I think, who answers his own question so prettily, but I remember the rhymes only, and not easily the rhymer. Certainly my bird is no nightingale, for there are none in this well-farmed plain without woods or thickets to invite them. A lingering and eloquent thrush it must be, up late in the fine weather.

For the nearest nightingales I know of are up in the hills, in a rough tangle of bracken and bushes which stretches for miles over hummocky ground. And there they sing all day, as well as (I suppose—for I have never stayed to see) all night. They have an astonishing range of voices, from the real true prima donnas to humble performers as harsh and scratchy as the old Gramophone and records I bought in a sale for the children to play for themselves.

But, good or bad, the singers are always "she," so firmly have the poets and the Greek story-tellers imposed their romantic conceptions on the facts of our natural history. And her voice for me is not so much "ravished" as—fruity is the word I want, for all its associations of fat contraltos and well-dined men with cigars. Rich, mellow, eloquent—but fruity is better. And there is one note, repeated with infinitesimal rises of tone, which is as exciting as the curlew's questioning call before it breaks into the longed-for final trill.

To me, at least, the rise of tone is almost indistinguishable between each note, but I can believe that to a musician with a sensitive ear the notes are quite clearly an ascending scale. For any of our scales can be only an arbitrary choice of certain notes which the human ear can distinguish as different in a range of sounds whose gradations are far too minute for us to make out. A sensitive instrument would no doubt record a dozen separate notes between what seems to us the merest shade of flatness or sharpness.

She makes, the nightingale, a really quite astonishingly loud noise with her "little instrumental throat." Did Izaak Walton hear her as fruity too, I wonder, and was his instrument a cello?

One day soon we must go up into the hills and see if they are back. We will go for a picnic, which does not mean that I must struggle with baskets of food and thermos flasks, but only, it seems (for the children make the rules), that I must sit down and stay in the same place while they play, and that we must eat *something*. A pocketful of biscuits will do, so we will go lightly the next fine day, and look for the nightingales. I do not know when they come back here for the Summer, only that by the beginning of April they are singing everywhere in the Camargue, as common as sparrows in that strange, flat country.

And here tonight my thrush sings and sings. The air is very still, with scarcely a movement to carry the hawthorn scent in waves over the house. And quiet, so that the bird singing a field away sounds as clearly as across water. It is odd to think that this same quiet air is noisy with the whole world's wireless programs—earnest, vulgar, busy, pretentious, loud. That if we had the right (or the wrong) sort of antennæ, we should be deafened by a dozen orchestras all playing at once, chattered at in a score of languages, utterly distracted. But because we are insensitive lumps, we hear only the thrush dropping its tunes lazily into the quiet.

It would be interesting to have bird-songs recorded by an instrument not deaf, as human ears are, to the high notes. For in the songs of many birds, especially the warblers, there are very high notes almost too high to hear, like a squeaking pram-wheel. Even the husky-voiced whitethroat has occasional high squeaks, and probably there are other even higher notes which we do not hear at all, making of their calls a completely different pattern from the one we know. The willow-wren's indeterminate song might not sound like a wistful minor version of the chaffinch's bouncing tune, like a wood-nymph imitating a hockey-captain.

The warblers have been back for weeks now, and to-day the turtle-doves are here, calling on all sides with their contented but faintly melancholy prrr—prrr— They always arrive within a few days either way of the last week of April, but generally exact; and they come, not in odd stragglers, but all at once. This must be good country for them, for they are everywhere, a steady far-off chorus throughout the Summer, and in Autumn, when the corn is carried, they fly up in small flocks of striped tails, ten or twenty together, whenever we go through the rick-yard and disturb them among the haystacks.

One day when I was lying in the orchard, a turtle-dove settled low in the tree above my head. It was so close that I could see the red rim of its round bird's eye, and watch the sheen on its feathers when it moved. For once I felt like Gilbert White, who, not hesitating to shoot any bird which interested him, describes even the shyest and rarest in such tantalizing detail, distinguishing precisely between greenish-yellow and yellowish-green.

After a time my turtle-dove began to sing, and between each lovely prrr—prrr—was a little fussy quack, as domestic as a duck's. Well, Gilbert White would not have heard that by shooting, nor seen the absurd way it jerked its head at the same time. But still they are the most evocative and magical of the fine-weather birds, and no Summer would be complete without their mournful purring. Nor without the wood-pigeon's diving Summer flight, as if from time to time, in "the rolling level underneath him steady air," they came to some invisible cliff and jumped over. "Clack." Their wings meet above their back like a diver's hands, then down they go, a steep and graceful swoop before they recover and fly on again.

> *Come now, and leave your city chair,*
> *Where pavements batten down the flowers,*
> *To lie in grass for hours and hours,*
> *And watch the ring-doves dive in air.*

How upsetting a new relationship is, and how like travelling without a map in a strange land. At the beginning of a new acquaintance, every meeting is a voyage of discovery, and the view may turn into quite different country as we walk into it. The person we say good-bye to is not at all the one we met an hour ago, the vistas have changed as we travelled, the emphasis shifted, so that we know we too must have changed equally for them, but do not in the least know how. Are they pleased with us, or have we disappointed them? Have they found in us only blind patches, or unexpected understanding? We need so badly to be reassured at the beginning. Simply a postcard will do in the next morning's post, or a formal note saying thank you for the evening. And even in the intervals of meeting there are changes. For everyone we are separated from, even for a day, is a slightly different person when we meet again. We must make an imaginative effort to assimilate their new experience which we have not shared.

Yet it is not only that each must get to know the other, but that we ourselves are a different person in every relationship. The person Jack thinks us to be, and the person Jill knows, are no more alike than Jack and Jill themselves, and the relationship itself creates a new personality, as colours change under different lights. So that the early meetings are like trying to sing in tune without knowing what the tune should be, having to find it out for ourselves by listening for the discords or harmonies in another person. It is a voyage of intimate exploration of *ourself*, as well as of the other, so that the most fascinating talk for any lovers is to tell each other of the beginning of their love.

Not that any of our changing is deliberate or even conscious. It is only when the relationship is firm and easy that we realize suddenly, one day, how the self which goes to one meeting would not at all do for a different one, that there are people we cannot meet together. Yet it is nothing to do with deception, only the chameleon quality of women, of unconsciously becoming what is wanted of them. And it is why too, if we are to distil any personality of our own, we must be so much alone.

And how absurd my own personality becomes, so much distilled alone out here. Today in the library I picked up a book called *The Inner Ear* and was disappointed to find a medical text-book when I had expected an anthology of esoteric poetry.

This house, like the greatest works of art, has a strange poetic power of intensifying experience and making it somehow significant. From our humdrum lives it creates some ultimate relevance, some beauty perhaps, if it did not sound so precious; and so ridiculous too in this rou-time of housework and baby-minding. Yet from days of drab unhappiness is crystallized, for an instant, the very lyric essence of grief, the most ordinary pleasures blossom at moments into exquisite joy.

It is what Pater calls the "chief function of all higher education, the art of so relieving the ideal or poetic traits, the elements of distinction, in our ordinary life—of so exclusively living in them—that the unadorned remainder of it, the mere drift and debris of our days, comes to be as though it were not."

There is a drift and debris in plenty, the elements of distinction are rare and unpredictable in the unadorned remainder, the telephone interrupts them, the milk boils over, the children quarrel and must be sorted out. But still, despite the trivialities, there is this poetic transmutation of our lives by the house itself, as if one gave some ordinary idea to a great artist, who lived it back superbly through oneself. It is not our doing, it happens despite ourselves, and I think it will happen nowhere else.

Even the children feel it, though puzzled and inarticulate, struggling to express themselves in the inadequate words they command. Peter today came in thoughtful and dreamy. "I was walking round the orchard. I was looking at the juicy grasses." Then he stopped, gazing through the kitchen window with unseeing eyes, hesitated, and said it over again slowly, then stopped again. A long struggle to get so ephemeral and dazzling an experience into common counters. Then out it came in a rush. "I was walking round the orchard. I was looking at the juicy grasses. I was sit-downing under a tree, and the sun came out, and I was *very* happy."

PART THREE

SUMMER

P ERHAPS IT IS TRUE, AS I HAVE ALWAYS
wondered, that we love best the season of the year
which is nearest our own season of life. For I have
reached June now, I suppose, with the first flowering
over, and my children growing steadily like the small
green apples in the orchard outside the windows. And it
is June now that I love best in all the year.

It is a strangely secret month, with the birds hidden in
thick leaves, and the fields of mowing-grass and green
corn untrodden and mysterious. No one has crossed
them, for there would be tracks to show, only the small
animals which live their private lives among the forest
of stalks. Even the stream is lost in a green tunnel of willows, like the brook of the Ancient Mariner (that but-
tonholing bore of an old man who really should never
have been allowed into the party to bother the wedding
guests with his moralizing):

SUMMER

A noise like of a hidden brook
In the leafy month of June,
That to the sleeping woods all night
Singeth a quiet tune.

This is Keats's Summer, a "land of fragrance, quiet-
ness, and trees and flowers," for Keats more than anyone
else describes this lushness of the early season:

In deepest grass, beneath the whisp'ring roof
Of leaves and trembled blossoms, where there ran
A brooklet, scarce espied:
'Mid hush'd, cool-rooted flowers fragrant-eyed,

for the Spring fit of quoting is not yet over, it seems.

But the rest of Summer Keats never notices—the flies
which buzz against windows, the heavy trees in pools of
shade, and when the roads are hot and dusty, the mirages
of dark water which vanish before us.

For Keats, Summer is never social. He does not hear
the bands in parks, and how voices are different out of
doors. For him there is no orange-peel in public places,
no untidy picnics on his hills. Who could ever guess he
lived by Hampstead Heath?

Yet the end of Summer is a social season, not a private
dream in meadows as June is. Even in the country there
are local shows in August, village fêtes and parties in
vicarage gardens, wearing out the Summer, wearing out
the lawns in bare patches which will not be green again
till the Autumn rains. And even the bare patches one
grows fond of, even the dusty feet and orange-peel and
flies on sweating horses, because they too belong to the
fine, high blaze of Summer weather.

Dear Peter, who talks about "this year's Summer" and

"last year's Summer," as if it were not an inevitable season of every year, but an unexpected treasure come to enrich his ordinary life. So it is, but much more. We become a different person in the Summer: become an extrovert after Winter's introspection—these awful words. In the fine weather we are free, not hampered by clothes, not confined in the house, so that even our movements are different, simpler and more gracious, not huddled against the cold. And living out of doors, we become more generous, more tolerant, less shut in and moody in the long daylight. Hieronymus Bosch, Strindberg, and the rest, come from lands where the Winter is too long. Their first effect always is to make us sigh for the sun.

Summer weather, like being in love, is a philosopher's stone which turns our ordinary days to gold. But not the whole day, whatever young people in love may hope. For it never is the whole day, never all our life which is transformed in any happiness, but only the exquisite moments. Looking back we remember a series of separate and complete occasions, not joined in any way by the intervening time, which we have forgotten. It is like first going to London, when we travel everywhere by Underground and get to know the great city as a collection of familiar but disconnected oases round the different stations. And at the time, living our life, being with the loved person, there is no way at all of telling which will be the remembered moments, which are the occasions we shall treasure always as inexplicable happiness.

"We love those we are happy with." I have wanted for years to know who said it, for it comes now to be one of the truths. When we were very young it seemed the wrong way round, an equation true enough in reverse, but pointless rather in the given order. We are happy with those we love; that, we thought, was the obvious truth. But when we were as young as that, we knew what we meant by loving, and happiness, we imagined, for we were very confident, must always follow if we got what we wanted. Living was difficult, but simple. And now the difficulties are more manageable, but nothing is simple any longer. Perhaps it is only to the young that things seem so, and we must, after all, grow up. We love those we are happy with. Yes. We do. For how else can we know we love them, or how else define loving?

RE-READING *As You Like It* for the leafy Summer, the greatest interest, though after the poetry always, is in the different patterns of homosexuality, which I never noticed till now.

First Rosalind and Celia, obvious and accepted. Their loves, says someone or other, "are dearer than the natural bond of sisters."

> *We still have slept together,*
> [It is Celia speaking now]
> *Rose at an instant, learn'd, play'd, eat together,*
> *And wheresoe'r we went, like Juno's swans,*
> *Still we went coupled and inseparable.*

Celia is the gentle one, the clinging and affectionate girl—"I cannot live out of her company," she sighs. And Rosalind is not only, as she says herself, "more than common tall," but more than common boyish—active, sprightly, quick-witted, mischievous, bold. She can be very tiresome. She puts on doublet and hose with obvious relish, and with quite natural ease plays the pert boy with the love-lorn Orlando. It is easy enough to see who will rule the house when they are married and happy ever after. For though Orlando may be more than a match

for Charles the strong fellow, he will never for a moment
stand up to Rosalind.

The second pattern is the relationship between Orlando and Ganymede disguised. Half innocent, half mischievous, with fascinating overtones of meaning for the
sophisticated audience it was written for, as if they
watched children making gestures whose significance the
children did not understand, but the audience did.

Then there is Phoebe in love with Rosalind disguised
as a boy. We are in the secret, and so is Rosalind, and she
is more delighted than embarrassed, for, as all through
the play, her reactions are ambiguous.

For the Elizabethan audience there was also the constant suggestive twist that the women's parts were played
by boys. So that if the hero makes passionate advances to
his lady (or perhaps even more if the villain does), it is
always a boy he is addressing, some exquisite page of a
boy with a girl's voice. And it is surely naïve in us to see
it as simply ridiculous, to suppose the Elizabethans were
not conscious of this added piquancy of a boy acting the
part of a girl disguised as a boy. Certainly Shakespeare
who wrote the sonnets must have been very conscious of
the charm.

"There are times," I thought, for the night was warm
and troublesome, "when only to walk round the garden
is to suffer an onslaught of emotions and associations almost too intense to be borne. It is nothing to do with happiness or unhappiness," I said, "but that all feeling, at
this pitch of intensity, is pain. Pain scarcely endurable
when one is not any sort of artist, and cannot communicate the experience. Cannot say it, or paint it, or
sing it out, being nothing at all expressive, only a boat
with too much sail and scarcely enough ballast."

But what nonsense it all seems in this morning's sun with the sparrows domestically chirping. Emotional on-slaughts indeed! The slugs have eaten my seedlings in the night, and it serves me right. Besides, I must mow the lawn.

But the view of one's life changes under the emotional light like any other landscape. The storms are as authentic as the clear weather, and last night's enchanted garden as real as this morning's lawn-mower. We can no more take the view neat and complete without the viewer than we can pack up light in boxes. Though even that used to seem possible enough, for I would sit for hours as a small child, trying to pull down the blind fast enough to trap the light in the room before it escaped through the window.

The lawn is covered with drifts of daisies like surf over flat sands, and I lie beside the mowing-machine, looking along their level heads, and think of reasons why I should not cut them down. That the lawn could not look more delightful. That it is cruel to the daisies, Peter thinks, and so do I, daisies having still the same trusting and innocent eye that they had for me as a child. Then newly mown lawns in small gardens have an unfortunate suburban air; one needs a great sweep of turf for it not to look neat merely. Besides, it might be easier to get to like the grass long than to cut it down every week, more philosophic to accept things as they are than to struggle always to make them conform to one's own unreasonable ideas. For it is, after all, most unreasonable to insist on mowing grass which grows again the moment we leave it, as unreasonable as men who shave every morning their chins meant to be hairy.

Which is all true enough, but truer still (for as Rochefoucauld says, it is the reasons we never urge which are the real ones), truer that it is more pleasant to lie in the sun than push the mowing-machine.

So I lie among the uncut daisies and watch the children dancing round the lawn, dressed in daisy-chains and nothing else, like eighteenth-century cupids. "Self-conscious," I say, and they pick it up like a ball to play with. "Self-conscious, self-conscious, self-conscious." Hopping on one foot, then the other.

But suddenly they stop. "What does it mean? Self-conscious?"

"It's what you are now," I say, and they are satisfied. Self-conscious, they think, means wearing a daisy-chain, and back they go to their hopping. So now whenever they see a small girl adorned with daisies, they will say: "Look. She's self-conscious." And grown-ups overhearing will think how precocious they are, and how unkind.

And still I leave the growing daisies, and watch the children with idle pleasure. For Peter this Summer is a lovely child to watch, with movements of controlled grace and perfect attitudes. He stands in a doorway or leans against a tree, and always, unconsciously, it is a ballet-dancer's pose. John too is endearing enough, with his generous, smudgy face as if someone had moulded it with their thumbs; but it is a baby's charm, and will soon be over. Next year, indeed, they may both be plain, fat, and ugly perhaps, or thin and overgrown, and in five years awkward schoolboys with bony knees and feet too large.

But now Peter reminds me of the only love-affair of my co-educational school-days. I was sixteen, I suppose, and he was nine, for boys of the same age are too young for girls in their teens, or perhaps, looking back, it was I who was too young, an overgrown child. I used to see him when he sang in the school choir, a frail, exotic-looking boy with reddish, silky hair and transparent skin. How dear eccentric Cardinal Pirelli would have appreciated him.

He had fits of furious temper, they said, changing to a half-mad and menacing demon whom no one dared cross. But I longed to put him in a steamy hot-house, among orchids as tawny as his hair, and watch the strange evil blossoming of his tempers.

His sister was in my class, a pleasant, dull girl, but fascinating to me because she shared the life of so glamorous a creature. Yet I never spoke to him, only to his sister about him, his older sister who saw him only as a tiresome younger brother. He was spiteful, she said, and vicious, and impossibly spoilt. Of course he was, for that was part of his perverse charm. But he was beautiful too, which she did not see, and I was angry always to see him in shapeless grey flannel suits and hairy socks, so silken a purse to make into a sow's ear.

My school-days were a reasonably happy time, for being a depressingly serious child, I enjoyed the lessons and was only sorry there were not more. I made no particular friends, for I can scarcely have been the sort of person anyone would want to make friends with, but much more surprisingly, I made no enemies.

I was a good enough looking child, I suppose, though I never thought so, being embarrassingly tall among those small north-country children, and with a mop of obstinately short curls when I wanted plaits. But one day before I left school for good, the headmistress sent for me to come to her study. There was something she wanted to tell me, she said. She knew I had never thought of it. She felt she must speak to me. Yet still she hesitated. It was not easy to begin, she said, and so she went on and on, each of us growing more and more embarrassed.

It was not exactly the Facts of Life that she told me in the end. That she would never have gone into, being discreetly old-fashioned, nor would I have let her, being sufficiently informed. But did I know, she said, that I was pretty? And that for girls who were pretty the world was a Wicked Place?

It took her a long time to say it, and I, being completely unaware, gave her no help by understanding quickly. For it had never occurred to me that anyone might consider me pretty, nor was I so, I think, except with the bloom most girls have at that promising age. But very few latter-day girls, even the beauties, can have left school with such a mid-Victorian warning. I remember still when I left her, rushing to the cloakroom mirror to gaze incredulously at the face she had praised. "How odd," I thought. "How very odd. Is it really going to be like that?"

It was naïve in her, I suppose, to see a world of such simple dangers, but naïve too in me, staring in astonishment at my face in the mirror, for at seventeen one really should not be of an innocence to embarrass one's elders.

Among girls, long before seventeen, to be pretty is to be in some way an aristocrat, immune from the ordinary rules and penalties. So that I could admit quite openly to that most unforgivable of school heresies: that I hated games. Netball, hockey, cricket, tennis, I disliked them all. But hockey more than all the rest. Even now I can never see a child with a hockey-stick in the raw Winter weather without feeling my throat sore in sympathy that they must run up and down a muddy field, breathless in the cold. It is one of the very real privileges of being grown-up, that no one expects me to play ball-games any longer.

SUMMER

All this I showed at school quite openly, without bothering to conceal it; but they only looked at me sideways and said nothing at all. Yet if I had been a boy, they would have made my life as wretched as I certainly deserved, and no pretty face would have saved me. For I never stayed after school to practise, never cared who won the coveted Saturday match. Even in school-time games periods I slipped away whenever I could, to sit on the cloakroom radiator and read Sir Walter Scott. For, with H. G. Wells, he was my favourite at that time. Such a satisfactory lot of him there was too, a whole shelf-ful in the library. You only had to remember to skip the first chapter, which was history and dull, and after that you were launched on the river of the story and could not stop.

The happiest days of all were at this time. I remember them still as separate unclouded jewels of happiness which nothing could spoil. "Detached from him, yet very real," Pater says of Marius the Epicurean, "there lay certain spaces of his life, in delicate perspective, under a favourable light, and, somehow, all the less fortunate detail and circumstance had parted from them."

The house we lived in was a long way from school, so that I went each day on my bicycle, taking lunch with me. And sometimes in the Spring or Summer, on days of blue invitation, I would set out as usual, and come back at the proper time, but in between I had been, not to school at all, but out into the country.

The next day at school they would ask where I had been, and I would lie without compunction, looking them straight in the eyes. I had a headache, I would say, or I ate strawberries and was sick, the most unlikely accidents, which I took pleasure in inventing. They can scarcely have believed me, but whether they did or not, nothing was ever said. Like my schoolfellows, they looked at me hard, and left me alone.

Yet if they had punished me, I should still have done it, as perhaps they saw. For those days were so intense a happiness that I would have suffered with indifference a week of being kept in—a punishment, moreover, which always seemed to me inefficient, since they too must stay behind after school to sit with me, and without the over-riding compensation of a day of playing truant.

First of all, on those stolen days, there was the wicked exhilaration of pedalling off as fast as I could push, when the school-door had swallowed up the last of the conscientious. I was completely alone, I had eight whole hours ahead, I was so entirely free that no one even knew where I was. It was perfect. Is it the Chinese who say that only the gods can have a whole day completely free? Well, I felt I too was among the gods, being too happy for the human state. If I had known Mallarmé, I should certainly have said it to myself as I trod the pedals round, too excited to sit on the saddle: *"Le vierge, le vivace et le bel aujourd'hui."* For it would make a good cycling rhythm, and quite perfectly expressed what I felt on setting out.

> *Le bonheur est dans les champs,*
> *Cours-y vite, cours-y vite,*
> *Le bonheur est dans les champs,*
> *Cours-y vite, il va filer.*

But I did not know that either when I was at school.

Always, as soon as I was safely away, I would eat the lunch I had with me. Not at all from hunger, since I had only just had breakfast, but from a feeling that it disencumbered the day, freed it finally from the last ordinariness of the usual routine.

It was on these days that I came to know and love the country. I travelled for miles around, for an active child can go a long way on a bicycle in eight hours. I became so familiar with the trees and flowers that they were nearer and far dearer than any people. Nor was it only romantic sentiment, and "the wind on the heath, brother," though there was that too, of course. But I loved the flowers for themselves, and not only as a reflection of my own personality.

I saved up and bought Johns's *Flowers of the Field*, dear credulous Mr. Johns, who could not abide tansy pudding—"that nauseous dish," he says, when he should be telling us the number of stamens. I learnt to run down in a flora the flowers I did not know. I struggled with botany books on osmotic pressure and the history of flowering plants and the difference in structure between monocotyledons and dicotyledons. Horsetails, those shrunken survivors of the coal forests, were to me as fascinating as buried treasure, and if I could have gone to Kew to see the cycads, it would have been a journey into high romance. It still is, though dimly now, like a remembered excitement.

Geography was well enough, but why tell us always about people, when I wanted to know what *grew* in those countries with the remote-sounding names? And though the dinosaurs and eohippus were interesting, no doubt, what I really wanted to know was what the flowers were like then, long before man was born to see them. I was lost in wonder, being easily lost, that the plants we know are only one group in a series of experiments; that the earth has been covered with other preceding vegetations as complicated as our own, lost plants just as beautiful, as well adapted to the conditions they lived in. It was my first intimation of mortality, not for myself, but for my whole world; my first awed glimpse of the dreadful enormity of the universe, of our own insignificance.

But I found quite quickly that nothing bored people so immediately and completely as botany. It still does. It bores people only to be told the names of the wild flowers we pass in the hedges, even the mysterious fairy-tale names like enchanter's nightshade, an unexpectedly meek little flower, and viper's bugloss, which grows so thick here in a valley of the chalk that it looks like blue smoke rising from the hillside. Ploughman's spikenard, white helleborine, yellow archangel, true camomile—they have no intrinsic magic for most people, it seems, as words have in charms.

Each family of flowers—rose, daisy, buttercup—is like a theme of music, and the different species are variations on it. Many of them are simple enough: buttercups, celandines, marsh-marigolds, Winter aconites, Christmas roses. These clearly are all the same fundamental pattern, each enriching the others by the memory of its own variations. So that the greenish-white of Christmas roses takes on a moonlit quality when we remember butter-cups are so clear and sunshiny a yellow. And fat marsh-marigolds are even more satisfyingly sturdy because the petals of celandines are thin and tapered.

But sometimes the variations are too difficult to follow. A delphinium for instance, I can no more relate to a buttercup than I can make the swaying waltz-time varia-tion have anything to do with the stated theme in Brahms's variations on the "Saint Anthony Chorale."

Each family has its own personality. The Scrophu-lariaceæ, so odd and unexpected, are the intellectuals, for what could be more like an eccentric scholar than fig-wort? The daisies are plebeians always, however charming, and the rose tribe, if not perhaps the highest aristocracy, is certainly the folk of good family, with an unmistakable elegance and refinement even among the humblest: silver-weed that grows by dusty roads, and the tiny exquisite tormentil of my northern childhood Summers on the moors. The really dull ones are the Crucifers, such a family of bores that for once I sympathize with those who yawn even to hear a flower mentioned outside a West End flower-shop.

But then, since Wordsworth, the country has become altogether too earnest, too mixed up with God. Daffodils no longer now remind us of Herrick and his light loves, but of Wordsworth's pensive mood. Even

the little birds that sit and sing
Amidst the shady valleys,

even they, it seems, must now praise God.

"God made the country, and man made the town." What nonsense. Yet someone said it. Someone who had never lived among the never-ending work of a country year. For the English countryside is as artificial as any park. These smooth fields and tidy hedges, these close-edged woods are only here because men have made them, and work constantly to keep them. Left alone, the land would soon return to what Professor Tansley calls its climax vegetation. Alder woods I suppose it would be for this valley clay. First, hawthorn scrub breaking up the grassland, as it does already in neglected fields, then as the field-drains were choked, wet marsh with rushes. For our lane here, firm and dry enough now, is not for nothing still called Marsh Lane, and in undrained fields there are pools all Winter in the hollows, and rushes high and green even at midsummer. But the first marsh would fill up in time with dead vegetation, and alders grow, as they can with their roots water-logged, covering the vale with damp alder forests, the comfortable fields forgotten.

The chalk would grow tall beechwoods, mixed with ash and box and yew and holly. For already, now the vanished flocks of sheep no longer nibble down the seedlings, the grassy sheep-walks are invaded by hawthorn and white-beam, hazel and dog-roses, with beech saplings growing up in their shelter, ultimately to outgrow and smother the bushes and the grass. Only where the weathering chalk is bare on the steep escarpment would the short, flowery turf survive, dotted with juniper bushes, which love the sun. Small wonder that all the early settlements here, the camps and forts and old tracks, are along the edge of the chalk, where men could see to live.

The chalk-hills now have a curious vague melancholy hard to account for. There is something missing, you feel, something dead which should be alive, something lost. The country has the same indefinable sadness as sterile parklands which grow no crops, as houses without children. It is strangely haunting until at last you realize what it is. There is no water. The field-ponds have dried up, the lakes have shrunk, the running streams have gone from the empty valleys, for the water-table has sunk, leaving no surface water. The land is still shaped by the streams and rivers which once drained it, cutting steep rounded hollows between the little hills, carrying the water down the long gentle tilt of the chalk to London and the Thames. But the water-table is too low now even for streams in Winter. Perhaps it is because so much land between here and London is paved and built over with a great water-proof lid of habitation, running the rain into the sewers. Perhaps the artesian wells of London draw off too much water, draining the chalk deep be-

neath the London clay. Perhaps, even, the climate has
become drier. But whatever the reason, the stream-beds
now grow short turf instead of king-cups and forget-
me-nots, and only a few clumps of stunted sedge now
mark what must have been clear pools not so very long
ago.

Along the foot of the escarpment there are reservoirs, fed by the water which soaks through the porous
chalk until it is driven out in springs where it reaches the
impervious underlying clay of the Vale of Aylesbury.
But even since we came to this country, the level in the
reservoirs has sunk. The shallow ends are grown over
with rushes and feathery willows, there is more mud for
the wading-birds, the retaining dams show successively
lower rims of litter as the water sinks.

Since the escarpment which faces us over the plain
is the highest point of the hills, the water-shed must always have been there on the highest edge, and no chalk
streams can ever have flowed down to us from the hills,
but only arisen in springs at the beginning of the clay as
they do still, as the stream does which runs through the
orchard. So that the gaps in the escarpment where the
roads and railways pass were formed, not by rain-water,
but by melting ice. In glacial times the ice-cap, they say,
reached as far south as this escarpment, reached here and
no further. And as it melted, the dammed-up water
spilled over the edge of the hills, flowing into the plain
below, and wearing down such convenient gaps for our
present-day roads—Tring and Wendover and Princes
Risborough. "Princy Rizz" the children call it, at first
because it was the nearest they could say, but now for
fun and affection. And as the water overflowed, it carried
with it stones and gravel from the ice, so that opposite
each gap, just below the soil, there are beds of varied

pebbles, as smooth and polished by the churning ice which brought them as pebbles on the sea-shore.

It is strange, holding them in your hand as rounded as marbles, strange to realize what ages of wear it has taken to grind down jagged fragments of rock to this smooth simplicity. For the simple things are the most worked over, the hardest to achieve, as early languages are impossibly complicated, harsh and rugged, and the idioms of French conversation, so deceptively easy, are only worn down from the first awkward utterances by thousands of years of smoothing tongues.

Indeed it is always disheartening that to put down anything simply needs so long an effort of writing and rewriting. Doctor Johnson's involved periods, no doubt, came rolling out extempore, but there are endless worked-over versions before Burns reached the perfect simplicity of "My love is like a red, red rose."

The country here is chalk and cheese, for though the name may come from Dorset, our clay in the Vale has just as much the texture of unripened cheese as any soil further west. And only a mile or two away across the fields, the chalk-hills rise up steeply from the plain to their own quite different scenery.

The chalk country is like a sophisticated woman, elegant, self-controlled, naturally reserved. Delicate she is rather, restrained; nothing is prolific. The crops are thin like the soil they grow on, the grass short, the cows sparer than the herds on the rich pastures of the Vale. And everywhere there is the curious air of sophistication, in the shapes of the land, the little hills crowned with dark trees, the abrupt line of the woods cut short by the ploughed land in lovely sweeping curves. From the terrace of West Wycombe House there is no way to tell where the park ends and the country begins, so much has all the landscape the air of being developed by Capability Brown.

But the landed gentry have their own particular vegetation, as distinct as the chalk or clay. When the hedges are hung with traveller's joy you know you are on the chalk, but just as surely a cedar tree means the aristocracy are somewhere near. For no one else plants cedars, so long they take to grow, with their branches of planes superimposed, curiously dream-like. When the woods are varied with conifers, and evergreens run wild in the undergrowth, when the hillsides are decorated with clumps of trees, and there are vistas cut through the woods to the view beyond, then you know there will be a big house somewhere near. Even though it is a hospital now, the ancestral home, with only a cramped acre of garden, or pulled down perhaps and its very site forgotten, the family living in a London mews, still the country round has the air of a landscape garden. There are fences instead of hedges, specimen trees in the middle of fields where cows rub against them; still by remote and ghostly control the vanished great house keeps the countryside a park.

For the landed gentry (a charming old-fashioned name for an old-fashioned animal) have their own scenery as well as their own vegetation. The land has not been ploughed and levelled, but keeps its natural hills and hollows, accentuates them in the name of Salvator Rosa and the picturesque. There are ponds and impressive lakes in country which, left alone, manages only humble streams. There are no hedges, no undergrowth, but sweeps of open green between tall trees. And even the grass is different, not close enough for turf, not lush enough for mowing, but a special kind of discreet covering, looking from a distance like a kept lawn, dull to walk across, without flowers.

Yet much of the seeming parkland of the chalk is natural enough. Beech trees make the most controlled and tidy of woodlands, the usual tangle of undergrowth subdued in the shade beneath their close mosaic of leaves. And the untouched grassland of the naked chalk is as smooth and short as a lawn, inlaid with small, bright flowers which the butterflies love. It is naturally restrained and elegant country.

But leave the clay of the Vale alone to run wild, and in a year it is overgrown with nettles and thistles and the rankest weeds. It is a generous slattern only controlled by constant discipline. Yet in the Spring and early Summer the clay is at its best, as a woman without grooming is at her best in youth. Mile after mile of flowery meadows, great elms and solid banks of chestnuts, deep extravagant hedges, and grass too thick for the mowing-machine. Such a lavish cover of thriving green that we forget the soil beneath, as we never do on the chalk. It is like a household so wealthy that there is no consciousness of riches, only of ease and plenty, and the feeling that everything is there of its own accord.

It has its own delicacy, this heavy land. The constant willows and poplars of the well-watered clay give it the same lightness as the Impressionist landscapes, shimmering, always moving, more iridescent even than Monet painted them. Here, since it is not the land we look at but the cover of vegetation, the changing seasons transform the country, making a different world of Summer and Winter. But on the chalk we are conscious always of the bare bones of the land beneath the thin cover of green. Whether the trees are leafy or bare makes little difference, for it is sculptors' country, as the clay is a land for painters.

"*La chair est triste hélas! et j'ai lu tous les livres.*"

For it is June, and night, and troubled with what Shakespeare calls Summer's honey breath, and Auden more bluntly, the sexy airs of Summer.

Somewhere about our middle, the belly perhaps if it did not sound so Biblical, we harbour a blind creature who lives his own slow and secret life, parallel with our own quick conscious life of the mind. It is him we teach to walk and swim, to make love or ride a bicycle, and though he learns slowly, he learns for good. Even when we think we have forgotten in too-long intervals, he remembers his lesson without our caring, until we both die. We can still swim, however long we have avoided the cold English seas, still ride the bicycle rusting in the garage for the last ten years.

He knows exactly, unknown to us, all kinds of things we have never noticed: the feel of our bed, our usual chair, our old accustomed clothes. We are only conscious of his separate life when the bed is strange, the chair hard in the wrong places, the new coat tight under our arms.

He translates our fleeting and complicated emotions into his own slow sensory language. Sudden grief becomes a tingling in our finger-tips, excitement a shiver like moth-wings down our spine. We feel our mouth held tight and hard and know that we are irritated, or our face grown gentle when "the melancholy fit shall fall." Horror is a sharp pain in the back of our thighs, and happiness a delicious sensation that any moment we shall float up to the ceiling like a balloon. Worry brings a feeling of sickness, not in the throat like real nausea, but somewhere in the pit of our stomach, and sudden anguish is an acute pain in the soles of our feet, so that we curl our toes under to take the weight. That is always what I think of when the French say "*crispé d'angoisse*," of toes screwed up, and the bottoms of my feet sensitive with nerves I never suspected.

But it is a slower, smoother life than our thinking existence. The movements are not sudden, like intellectual reactions, but flow over us in a slowly mounting wave, as a muscle contracts when it is stimulated, not by the twitching nerve, but direct through its own slow fibres. So that we can wait, stepping off the edge of the pavement we had not noticed, jumping back from the suddenly approaching car, wait, knowing it will come, for the ache to start in the back of our neck and travel slowly down our spine and legs, leaving a chill in our back even at midsummer, and goose-flesh on our arms.

It is warm midnight, far too warm to sleep. Very still and near, and heavy with fragrance. The sad smell of roses, the warm smell of pinks, the smell of hot chocolate from the night-scented stocks under the window. It is what Stephen Spender would call "O night."

The moths come to my light and thud softly against the glass, their swift, heavy blundering curiously sensual. And since I cannot sleep, I have written six letters, six lots of paper covered with little crooked marks, to be shut away in secret envelopes and sent hurrying all over the world. And watching my pen writing a long way off, remote on the lamp-lit paper, I wonder just what it is we try to do when we write our letters.

We are not stating facts, which have no meaning half a world away. Not trying to set down the unattainable truth. But what? Trying really to reach another person. Not to tell them this happened or that, but to make them feel what it was like when these things happened, to make them share our life, because we are lonely. After all the passionate gestures of love, clasping hands is still the closest.

Certainly man is a new and different animal, and writing is a new sixth sense he has made for himself (though there are more than five already). But still such an imperfect sense. I watch the crooked marks coming from the end of my pen, and wonder what it is I am saying. Whatever it is, it will not be what I mean to say, for there are so many transitions between myself and the person I write to that what I want to say will arrive at the other end as no more than a distorted echo of my meaning.

First I must get it into words. But words are no more than symbols, approximations to our thoughts, abstract common counters, only vivid and alive in the hands of a proper writer. Then the reader must translate my symbols back into his own meaning and experience as best he may. It is as if we had a shopful of treasures which we would send our friends. We cannot send the things themselves, only the money they can be changed for, and with the money our readers must buy in their own shop the nearest equivalent.

And the nearest will be so very different. Not only because we are different people, feeling differently, thinking, even seeing and hearing in quite different ways, but for each of us, living separately, our experience is remote from the others.

"It rains and rains," I say, "and the children are cross." But they know nothing of cross children, they have nothing to exchange for my counters. And I have never felt the heat of their tropical Summers, never felt my mind become as idle and languorous as the body. "It is hot," they say. "Hot, hot," and I think only of sun-bathing in the garden.

Even the things we both share will not transplant out of their context. I write softly in the evening, but they read it crisply at breakfast, among the toast and the coffee and *The Times* propped up. And how can we even guess what other people hear us to be saying, unless we are with them and can watch the shadow of our words on their faces?

Still I shall send my letters, for I have never been strong-minded enough to put even the obviously unsuitable ones in the wastepaper basket. And besides, I have written every one of my six exactly to the bottom corner of the last sheet, leaving no empty page at the end, an achievement of delicate planning which I only sometimes manage to arrive at. But once upon a time a young man said that I must never send an empty page in a letter, that it was like turning someone back at the gate, when they had come all across England to see you. And it seemed so sad that ever since I have tried to fill my pages to the last corner.

Peter has no difficulties about his letters, no hesitations. Written or read, they are themselves and the same, life for Peter being still difficult but simple.

For the children have a new game, of dictating letters which I must write down and send to their friends.

Andrew, come to tea next Thursday. And come and see they are cutting the hay.
    With love from Peter.
    With love from Peter.
    With love from Peter.
Peter can't stop saying with love from Peter. It's so nice. Peter keeps saying with love from Peter every Winter.

Well, it seems friendly enough, although he insisted that he would not begin: "Dear Andrew."

"People always do," I said.

"No. I don't. When I see Andrew I don't say *dear* Andrew. I say Andrew. So I'll write just Andrew now."

READING Donne again after years, it is oddly now the sermons which are most satisfying, not the poems. Almost one can hear them, the sermons, rolling out in fear and glory through Saint Paul's, though not, I suppose, the Saint Paul's we know—"Mine enemy is not an imaginary enemy, fortune, nor a transitary enemy, malice in great persons, but a reall, and an irresistible, and an inexorable and an everlasting enemy. The Lord of Hosts himselfe. The Almighty God himselfe. The Almighty God himselfe onely knowes the waight of this affliction, and except hee put in that exceeding waight of an eternall glory, with his owne hand, into the other scale, we are waighed downe, we are swallowed up, irreparably, irrevocably, irrecoverably, irremediably."

It is sublime thunder. Sublime, but a long way off. It does not concern us. Yet there was a time, round about one's twenty-first birthday, when Donne was the only wear, when he spoke more vividly than any other, came back the three hundred odd years to talk intimately into our very ear.

But not any longer. He is brilliant still, and intellectually trenchant, it is a perverse pleasure to follow his strange wit, but he is no longer an essential part of the untidy bedside pile, as Milton's *Comus* is, and Bacon's *Essays*, and the *Maximes* of La Rochefoucauld. In the end it is gentleness he lacks, and it is hard to love him, even though he still talks of "windowy nets" and "men with gold and honey in their names." The charm in his writing belongs not to him, but to his period, that peculiarly intimate charm of the seventeenth century, coming clear and irresistible through the eighteenth-century urbanities, and the nineteenth-century revolutions, to our own strident and anxious muddle. The Age of Anxiety, Auden calls us, but the Age of Self-Pity would be almost truer. For, reading our twentieth-century literature, what may well strike the future most vividly is how sorry we all are for ourselves. All articulate childhoods are miserable, all adolescents misunderstood, all schooldays wretched. Young men are blighted by war, adults frightened and frustrated, the whole world out of joint.

Well, so it has always been for thinking people, and even nowadays there are no doubt thousands of happy children, millions of people as reasonably contented as they have ever been. But not in literature. It is not fashionable. For no age has ever concentrated on its woes as we do, crying out so persistently for pity.

Even in the old days when he was my favourite poet, Donne's views were disquieting.

Hope not for minde in women; at their best
Sweetnesse and wit, they are but Mummy possest.

It was discouraging to a hopeful twenty-one, for minde was quite exactly one's dearest delusion. Sweetnesse? No. One was not sweet. Too intolerant still, staring too ruthlessly and making no excuses. And as for wit, that, like Juliet and marriage, was an honour we dreamed not of. We were too earnest, too enthusiastic. Since our ideas still engulfed us, how could we hope to manipulate them into wit?

But what else could we offer so ruthless a critic, and what console ourselves with? A gleam of beauty perhaps, since it is a light which must shine on everyone at twenty-one, however fitfully, and since one's young men were always reassuringly flattering. But the compliments of young men are not a statement of fact, but of their own visions. And even though they may see us in beauty while the enchantment lasts, the person they are in love with must always be beautiful, and we are no more than the peg they happen to hang their dreams on. When young men tell us we are like trees and flowers and May mornings, or any of the other unlikely and charming things which young men do say, it is not because of any qualities in ourselves, but because the figure they fall in love with is always like that, and we are the nearest equivalent.

So one will always be snared by smooth hair, another by dimpled hands, not because the hair or the dimples are any expression of the person they happen to belong to, but because they are chance associations which invoke for the young man his romantic ideal.

One will praise us for being thin, another because we are plump, for though our weight has not changed by an ounce since we left school, their ideals incline respectively to fatness and thinness. One will admire our pale skin because he likes blondes, another our dark hair because he prefers brunettes, but neither will ask us what books we are reading, for they are not interested in us for ourselves, but only in their own reactions.

And Donne made it all quite sadly clear.

> *Twice or thrice had I loved thee,*
> *Before I knew thy face or name;*
> *So in a voice, so in a shapelesse flame,*
> *Angells affect us oft, and worship'd bee;*
> *Still when, to where thou wert, I came,*
> *Some lovely glorious nothing I did see.*

That was what one felt like, reading Donne. Mummy possest. Some lovely glorious nothing.

But young women should not trouble their shining heads about Donne. Such a waste it is for *"les Jeunes Filles en Fleurs"* to sit reading the dull dead. They should stand at the mirror and arrange new ways for their hair. For they do it with such grace, such a lovely gesture of lifted arms, swaying back a little from the waist. There is somewhere a tiny early Greek figure I once saw, with the exact poise. For it was charming, then as now it seems, to a different people thousands of years ago, the exact same attitude.

Hair and clothes for me then were still a tiresome necessity, as they are now to the children, and getting dressed a tedium helped out by a book propped open on the dressing-table. And one has no business to be so innocent at twenty-one, not on warm Summer nights with the air as soft as silk. For I sat newly bathed by the open window, idly reading Donne while I brushed my hair, more conscious of the wind on my damp skin than the familiar elegies. "Variety." There it was, the usual witty justification of flightiness, and "Love's Progress," a poem Donne would certainly burn, I thought, when he reformed later on. But no more, any of them, than literary exercises.

Then quite suddenly it happened. Happened as I turned over the page from one poem to the next. "Come, Madam, Come." It was a beginning much like any other, but not for me, not that particular Summer night with the wind blowing in warm at the window. "Come, Madam," he said in a voice dead three hundred years ago. "Come." And I came. Quite suddenly I realized for the first time what it was all about, this preoccupation of the poets with making love. For one can breed white mice at school, and read all the Restoration comedies, yet still be as grave and ignorant as the children, since knowing has, after all, very little to do with realizing.

So I read on, with every line and invitation more and more confused. "Off with those shooes," he said, but that really was too much. Too much, absurdly, even in a voice three hundred years a ghost, and, even though I had no shoes on to begin with, I shut the book in embarrassment, buried under a cushion that frontispiece of Donne's brilliant lascivious face, and wrapped myself up closely in a dressing-gown.

From then on, perhaps, my life should have been quite different, but it was not. Once dressed, I took the troublesome Donne from under his cushion, and holding him carefully for fear the pages should blow open again, I put him out in another room. Then went to bed and read Jane Austen's *Emma*, but conscious now, for the first time, of how very much she leaves unsaid.

Young women who read Donne are in many ways very backward, since it is the main function of the university to arrest the emotional life, to guard against all direct knowledge of the human world, lest it crowd out the life of the mind. For the world and the flesh we shall learn inevitably, and once learnt, they are all-engrossing, but the mind's activity is easily checked, and dies early.

This dark river of sex through the landscape was my greatest discovery since I had realized with anguished surprise, some years before, that all was *not* for the best in the best of all worlds. But I still dressed myself absent-mindedly, still took no trouble to arrange my hair, only watched the young men I knew as if they were a new kind of creature. I sat on the bank and looked at the river, not being, it seemed, either horrified at the fierce-

ness of the current, nor yet one of the spontaneous div-
ers-in, but only interested.

In the Victoria and Albert Museum there is a miniature
by Nicholas Hilliard (or by Isaac Oliver, for they keep
an open mind in true scholarly fashion), a portrait of a
young man against a background of flames. Cynical,
amused, involved, for me it is the face of the young
Donne. And I have a postcard reproduction of him
wedged always in the frame of my mirror, keeping him
there for old time's sake, and to save me, living out here
with the children, to save me perhaps from naïveté.

THE front meadow is yellow over with buttercups, and
the children come in a dozen times a day to shine them
under my chin and tell me I like butter. But the Farmer
does not like them at all; he must plough up the grass,
he says, and get the field clean of weeds before he plants
it again. And neither do the cows. They avoid all they
can for the bitter taste, and when the unavoidable buttercups go down with a mouthful of juicy grass, the milk
has a sourish taste and smell.

They are Persian flowers, Proust says, Eastern creatures, but for me they are wholly English, cheerful and
wholesome, so lavishly healthy in the lush grass that I
am glad of the cows as milk-making intermediaries between us and so much goodness.

The children play in the stream, and I lie and wonder,
between long pauses of complete idleness, what sense
and medium could best evoke this world of early Summer. It depends, I suppose, on one's kind of memory. If
we remember in sounds, the *Pastoral Symphony* perhaps,
or birds singing over a hedge, and the ebbing, flowing
rattle of hay-cutting in the next meadow. If we remem-

ber in pictures, as most people do surely, there are orchards by Camille Pissaro, and Monet's gardens, though he is too formless to be one of my own favourites. Van Gogh's Summers will not do at all, not even the cornfield lark—they are too hot and fierce for our soft, leafy season. Nor will the little shrubby hill behind Christ in Piero della Francesca's *Baptism*, it will not do for England, however much it may seem the very abstract essence of Summer.

But a dry pressed daisy may be all we need, or a tiny green beetle closed into a book, for it takes only the slight right touch to evoke the whole remembered Summer world. And some poets can do it. For me the mediæval lyrists, and Spenser, and early Milton, and sometimes a phrase of Keats, though his is rather a Pre-Raphaelite picture of Summer than Summer itself. And Shelley is no use at all. "Moonlight-coloured may" indeed. Keats's "White hawthorn" is much nearer the solid, prickly reality. Though it was Shelley who said: "parsley green in its own light" (or was it white after all?).

Perhaps we could remember by touch, warm wind through cotton frocks, or the feel of mowing-grass against our legs, not in the least "soft as the breast of doves," not "shivering-sweet" either, but whippy rather, like running a stick along railings.

Or perhaps by smell, this general sweet floweriness, like the belch of damp fragrance which engulfs you on warm days going into the tents at the Chelsea Flower Show, and which I looked forward to every year.

But how delightful if only there were some way of conjuring up this green felicity on a drear-nighted December. And what time it would save us, holidaying in June. Like des Esseintes in *À Rebours*, who felt he *must* go to England. So he packed his bags and set off. But sitting in the English restaurant in Paris, he became so saturated with the atmosphere of all things English, the tweeds and the china-blue eyes and the women with large teeth, that he felt he had already been, and turned round and went home again satisfied, back to his ventriloquist and his horrible violent pictures, and the house haunted by the perfume of frangipane.

And I lie in the sun enjoying the pleasure, equally as perverse as his, of being too hot to bear it another moment, a pleasure only spoilt because I cannot purr with contentment like a cat.

What a pity it is that we cannot suggest minor improvements in ourselves, as car-fanciers do for their cars. There are so many small conveniences I would like arranged another time. There is the purring. Then I should like eyelids thick enough to lie flat in the midday sun without dazzling. I should like ear-lids for my ears, or at least to be able to listen only in the direction I wanted to, like seeing. I should like legs short enough not to stub my knees on the bus seat in front. I should like the skin of my hands to be two or three times thicker, so that it did not literally wear away when I start spring-cleaning. I should like long hands, which are useful, not to go so logically with long feet, which are not. For I can never read a novel about a heroine with long, thin hands (as all heroines seem to have) without fidgeting all through to remind the author that she will have equally long, thin feet, which, of course, are never mentioned. She will take size eight in shoes, and will need them made to measure to get them narrow enough. And unless she does, her shoes will fly off when she runs so gracefully down the garden path, and stay behind in the mud when she goes romantically walking in the wet woods. And since the war began, no one any more will make shoes to order. My shoemaker, who scorns women and their vanities, is delighted to insist that now he is only allowed to make Army boots. And I am left to manage precariously with only a single pair of shoes which fit. In the Winter I wear gum-boots, and in Summer bare feet, and when I go to London I carry my precious narrow shoes across the fields and put them on at the station, like the peasant girl in the story.

So I would like my feet fat. And I would like my nervous reflexes slow enough to give me time to control the starts and terrors at nothing at all, at a sudden slight noise, at coming on someone unexpectedly round a corner. Above all, I should like not to mind the cold so dreadfully, so that in Winter I need not wear so many layers of coats and jerseys that my elbows will not bend and my arms hang away from my sides like a doll's.

All this without what the doctors would call cosmetic improvements. As to that, of course, one could endlessly elaborate. But quite simply, if I could choose what I would look like, it would be the twelfth-century Khmer head with three faces in the Guimet Museum in Paris.

What is your substance, whereof are you made
That millions of strange shadows on you tend?

That is how women should look, even though they need not have three faces to deepen the mystery. And then, as Benedick says: "her hair shall be of what colour it please God."

And young men? Well, for them the details matter even less. What in them is most engaging when they are very young is a certain air of easy splendour, of being, not humdrum mortals, but glorious creatures come down to earth for their own amusement. I only knew them so at the university, though I suppose they must live somewhere else as well. Spoilt they were perhaps, handsome sometimes, not very intelligent, rich, I suppose, for certainly they took all good things for granted as their birthright. But when they were also nice people underneath, they had an easy grace, an aura of golden glory which girls know nothing of.

Out in the world they might have seemed carelessly arrogant, selfish perhaps, not worth the price of all the hard-working lives which earned their privileges. Certainly their quite unconscious magnificence would have perished, like exotic flowers too much handled. But in the rich, sheltered garden of the university they seemed the noblest of God's creatures.

And like a perfume, their easy splendour increased when they were together. The world they lived in became not only real, but the only life which mattered. Which was why I never wanted them to take me off alone on the river, where their glory faded and they became ordinary awkward young men, the only difference between them and commoner clay that they managed a punt with such effortless skill.

I liked them best in groups together, with me forgotten in a corner, so that they chattered among themselves, the paragons, of ski-ing at Christmas, and rowing blues in Spring, and what new mad place they should sail their boats to in the Summer. Above all, I liked to walk about the town between two of them (it never seemed much to matter which two, for I was in love with them all) while I half listened as they talked together over my head. For though I was tall, they seemed always to overtop me, bigger than life-size like the gods they were. And I would walk between them, dizzily happy to move in their reflected glory.

I suppose if John and Peter ever reach the university, this will be as lost a race as the even more unlikely dinosaurs. No one any more will have this easy golden splendour, and though I know it has gone to build rows and rows of good council houses, it is still sad that it has vanished. Sad that stirring cream and skimmed milk together makes only milk, and not all cream as the enthusiasts hopefully imagine.

But never mind. Peter has already found his own enchantment, for he has fallen in love with the girl in the village shop. He likes her hair, he says, and told me all about it in a charmingly apologetic way. He likes me *very* much (he assured me of this three times before he went on), but he does not much like my kind of hair. He likes hair to be either straight and "pale-goldy" (his own) or long and curly and "a sort of dark brown but a bit red," like the girl's in the shop. Well, I hope I shall still remember when he brings home a mouse-coloured fiancée.

But mothers are always uncordial, to say the least, towards their sons' young women. First they are suspicious, and half contemptuous too, of this stranger pursuing their desirable son. Then, when they realize it is the son himself who pursues, and not the young lady, they are guarded and a little frightened. When sooner or later she has said no, they dislike her whole-heartedly and without reserve, as if she had deliberately insulted them in doing what after all they wanted from the start, and not marrying their treasure.

Even at the time, without separating the stages, I knew that the mothers were never my friends. Do they then forget completely the various young men they too must have refused before they at last decided? The noes they must all have said before they said yes, since it is, after all, our only way of choosing?

But no doubt by the time Peter brings home his first love, I too shall be blindly on the side of the mothers.

It has been a still, soft day of indeterminate rain, the most intimate of country weather. For we are not closest to our friends the morning they win a sweepstake or get engaged to be married or otherwise rejoice, nor to the country on triumphal days of sun and wind and hard blue skies, hearty impersonal weather like a film star's smile showing all her teeth.

On the way to bed the children found a triple rainbow, a brilliant sweep over the barn roof, with a faint echo above and below against the purplish sky. A pretty conjuring trick which exactly suits them. But really rainbows are too theatrical. Too bright and obvious and mechanical. They are unworthy of the delicate contrasts of stormclouds and watery sun which beget them, the long smudge of the rainy hills, and the landscape softly divided into receding planes by the falling rain, like a Chinese painting. Mathematically exact, so that one imagines the point of a huge pair of compasses somewhere underground, neatly coloured like the spectrum we were taught at school, rainbows belong to the shiny illustrations of children's books. Only sometimes, when they come to earth so close that the trees and fields show beyond as unlikely as stage scenery under coloured lights, then they have the same iridescence as dragonflies' wings.

I remember being told, long ago, that you could only see rainbows after midday, and I still do not know whether it is true or not, only that the ones I notice are always in the evening.

Because it was wet and there were no customers in the
town, I bought this morning at a market stall a great arm-
ful of white lilies for a shilling. No one will buy them,
they said, because they bring death into the house. But
this house protects us from more powerful spells than
lilies. And now they stand, the whole lot of them, in a
deep stone jar under my window. And all day I have kept
the door shut to enclose their heavy fragrance, only for
the pleasure of opening it at last on to air so overwhelmingly sweet and drugged. And sitting in their scent, as
strong now as an anæsthetic, I have read *Romeo and
Juliet*, that play of a southern Summer night. For though
I suppose some of it must have happened by daylight, the
scenes we remember—the Capulets' feast, the orchard,
the tomb—these are all set in the warm Italian darkness.

But really *Romeo and Juliet* is a quite gratuitously
bawdy play. Not from nastiness like *Tristram Shandy*,
but from *joie-de-vivre* simply. Only a prude could mind
it, or a young girl. For when we are young—at least
when English girls are young (for others may be less
naïve)—we do not realize that romantic love need not
always be high-minded, that young men's lewdness is a
high-spirited joke among themselves, and not simply dis-
respect to young ladies. If the Nurse asks Romeo the
time (though I think it was his friend Mercutio) and he
answers so surprisingly, it does not mean that Romeo's
romantic passion for Juliet is only make-believe. It means
that roses must have their roots in good dung if they are
to bear the best flowers. The bawdiness gives warmth and
reality to their trance-like love, exists side by side with
the lovely formal poetry of conceits in the orchard, the
warm nights in Verona streets, and the young men with
torches, laughing and singing down the narrow lanes between the high garden walls, through the moonlight and

the nightingales and the scent of flowers. And the songs
they sang were quite certainly low songs, for the songs
of young men always are.

WE all of us pass our lives shut in the prison of our own
personality, each in his own separate cell of solitary con-
finement. And we look out, not to a clear outside world,
but to a version of it distorted by our prejudices and de-
sires and neuroses. We can never see things as they exist
in themselves, never know what really happens, only accept our own impression of what we think the world is
like, of what seemed to us to happen.

So in a story told us by another person, we recognize,
not the abstract fact, not truth, but the personality of the
teller. If objective reality exists, we can never know
more than a vague approximation to it, however clear our
minds. For Van Gogh's chair tells us more about Van
Gogh than about the chair, and our individual visions of
the world, if we had any objective standard to decipher
them by, would tell us more of ourselves than of the
world outside us.

Even the windows of our prison are inadequate, the
senses which are our only communication with the world.
We hear only a small range of the sound in the air; we
smell and feel very little; we see, even though man is a
seeing animal, only what is not too small or too large, too
near or too far, too dark or too light. It is as if we saw the
world in the half-light through a distorting mirror, heard
it faintly on a bad wireless-set. And for each of us our
individual distortions must be reality. We are imprisoned
for life. The sweep of half England from the picnic hill
is no more to us than a view from our cell window.

But there are rare moments after long tranquillity

when the prison walls grow thin and dissolve, when for a second or a lifetime—it makes no difference, for the experience is timeless—we feel direct contact with the outside world, experience it not as a stimulus which affects us, but as a very part of ourselves. It is a way of perceiving, as much more immediate than our ordinary senses, as suddenly seeing the light must be for a blind man who has only heard it described.

And sometimes it happens, on still Summer evenings when for hours there has been no sound or movement, but only a slow mellowing of the light. Sometimes one escapes. Escapes oneself. Feels one's mind grow upward like a branching tree into the quiet, roofless air, spread like fine seaweed in still water. One *becomes* the evening scene, not simply sees or hears it. One *is* the slanting light across the barley-field, and the smell of stocks, and the cold rising in the shadows.

But at the slightest disturbance, a voice from the farm perhaps, the telephone bell, or only the dog coming to be patted, at the least interruption you are back in your prison like a snail in its shell. You are yourself again, yourself who do not like the colour of the new barn roof, who are annoyed that the children are still awake, who cannot walk round the garden without thinking that the grass needs cutting and you are tired.

At other times on these long Summer evenings, in the particular hushed peace of places where children have been put to bed, sometimes this house breathes a mood of gentle, clear-eyed melancholy almost as sweet as pleasure. The late sun shines in the windows, the garden is full of birds, yet still it is sad, like a forsaken park, a quiet ghost. It is the same wistfulness as when a welcome person leaves the house, a lost unhappy feeling before it all settles back to ordinary life and the small everyday events take on again their usual significance. Limbo surely must have felt like this.

Well, the house is haunted, the villagers say. No one would live here, they tell us, until we came, and even now no one from the village will come out to us after dark. But there are no human ghosts here, only and always the house itself; a strange brooding presence, serenely benign, but with fear sometimes at night, blowing in from the trees like a dark wind, to scatter the vulgar and inessential. For the house in every inch of its fabric is overwhelmingly itself, and it is odd that so still and passive a personality should dominate all the generations of active people who have lived here, leaving no trace.

It was built in the sixteenth century, at the end of the Middle Ages, and still holds in its very bricks their Springtime consciousness of birds and flowers. The *Records of Ancient Monuments* dwells lovingly on its moulded cross-beams and inglenook and the great central chimney soaring like a tree from the hilly roofs.

It was mellow, the house, from half a century of seasons when Hamlet first declaimed aloud his rather stagey introspection. It watched the civil bitterness of the seventeenth century, and belonged then to John Hampden, for this was the farm, they say, for which he refused to pay Ship Money. His followers came here, perhaps, to hide in the secret room. Perhaps their bones are still there among the dust and spiders, but if so, their ghosts never trouble us. Even the eighteenth century did not presume to hide so mature a personality of a house behind a classic façade, not even so much as a pillared porch at the front door, and their raucous religious revivals could only sound ridiculous in so wise and tolerant an atmosphere.

The Victorians indeed, blindly confident in what seems to us for the time being their own bad taste, shut off the inglenook behind a great mahogany mantelpiece and covered the oak and plaster indiscriminately with violent rose-swagged wallpaper. But the house has shed such absurdities in a high bonfire in the orchard, and if it finds our whitewash and pale birch furniture from Finland equally incongruous, it at least does not seem so to me, and as the house will survive us by so many generations, it can tolerate our passing fashions.

The last to live here was a young roué, an engaging drinker and gambler straight from late nineteenth-century melodrama. He gambled away not only all his own money and all he could borrow, but even the cows and carts and ploughs, and when there was nothing left movable on his farm, he staked the very trees round the house. The great stumps are still there along the moat, sending up every year a forest of elm suckers, which every year I cut back to keep the view over the barley-field. But even the elms were not enough (for what do they make besides coffins?), and his creditors turned him out of the farm. He went away to work as a hired labourer, not in the least contrite, with no idea (thank goodness) of reforming, but only to get drunk on beer instead of spirits, to gamble more modestly on dominoes.

And the house lives on in its orchard, serenely indifferent, as it will be still, equally indifferent, when we too go away into the ordinary disenchanted world. Only sometimes, when the rooms are full of flowers, and the garden full of toys, and the children call to each other through the open windows, I feel the house is glad to have us, and not that we are simply another intrusion on its dreaming peace.

It is strange to realize that if we went away now the children would remember nothing of their life here but odd glimpses and occasions. For looking back to one's own childhood, it is difficult to sort out what we genuinely remember and what we have only vividly imagined from hearing it described. Any obvious event is almost certainly a reconstruction, for the occasions which are important for a child are very rarely the obvious events. It was in our own mind that things happened, not in the outside world. Scenes were trivial or important by some chance value of our own development, not by the values of the adult looking on.

But some things we remember so entirely from a child's point of view that no one else could ever have described them for us. For me there is a garden, wild and enormous, with a high wall at the end like the ramparts of the world. I remember still, though I could scarcely have put it into words at that dumb age, the feeling that over the wall was the great wide world where anything might happen. And in the garden grew trees as tall as tufted palms, with the sky overhead between their green branches.

The reality was a little walled-in back garden full of Brussels sprouts, and because we left it when I was sixteen months old, I suppose I never walked above them, my palm trees, but always crawled among the stalks on all fours, with the leaves meeting above my head.

Then at some time or other, without any context whatsoever that I can remember, there was a moment of dreadful tragedy in a flowery meadow. For a man walked past, trampling on the daisies and *not caring in the very least!*

No horrors since have so bitterly oppressed me with human cruelty. I followed him across the field, longing to kill him dead, and sobbing like a stormy sea. I still remember the great heaving breaths. I crossed the field behind him, standing the injured daisies up again, and certainly crushing a hundred myself for every one of his, like a cynical latter-day parable. Of the poor innocent offending man I saw nothing at all but a great pair of black boots with buttercup pollen yellow in the creases and a loop of tape at the back to pull them on with.

Then at some other time there was an imaginative grown-up who brought me a large red rose—a deep secret red it was, shading to black on the curve of the petals. It was for me certainly, but first I must climb on the table and recite nursery rhymes. Well, we lived in a flowerless city, and I loved flowers above all else. I would have jumped off the roof for that rose if they had asked me to. Better that, even, than the searing indignity of having to behave like a circus animal and recite on the table. Yet it seems a reasonable enough request to ask a small girl to recite "Little Bo Peep," and I can only hope that I was not always such a fiercely unpleasant child. For I recited my piece in a fury, jumped off the table hoping I should kill myself to spite them, snatched the rose, and locked myself in my bedroom. I scarcely think they can ever have brought me another flower.

I must have been four by then, yet I remember nothing at all of the background of my life, even though my father came home from sea, and we changed house and spent a whole Summer at the seaside. For so they tell me. I remember nothing except learning the trick of going to sleep as I walked along holding someone's hand, and of being able to fly downstairs simply by sliding my right hand down the banister. What we never remember at all is the boundary between dreams and waking.

W E have spent the Summer afternoon idle and happy in the children's play field, a narrow strip of grass with the stream on one side, and on the other a deep hedge as far through as a forest. It is here, in October, that we gather the best blackberries on all the farm. Because it is an awkward shape, and because the ground is uneven, sloping down to the stream in sudden ridges, nothing is ever done with this half-acre or so of meadow. The Farmer has given it to the children, and they call it their play field.

The little humps which defy the plough and the mowing-machine are perfect for rolling down, the stream here is deep and mysterious, and there are new flowers, water forget-me-nots and monkey-musk along the water edge, and a dozen different toadstools in odd corners. There is the great hedge to keep us from the wind, a sycamore tree against the sun like Izaak Walton, and an old dead tree-trunk where a green woodpecker nests, so oddly exotic a bird in an English field.

And here Charlie comes to visit us, splashing across the stream to find out what we are doing, curious, stupid, benign. For Charlie is one of the farm horses, the biggest horse I ever saw. Once he belonged to the railway yard and shunted five-ton trucks, as easily, I should think, as the children's toy trains. And ever since, like the popular heroes, he Doesn't Know His Own Strength. If he rubs against a gate-post, as horses do, the whole fence collapses. If he leans on his stable door, the bolts fly off, and out he comes clattering into the cobbled yard with the oddest air of astonishment. No one could climb on his back without a ladder, nor, once up, bestride him any more than an elephant. He could carry a palanquin, or six standing cowboys like a horse in a circus.

"Charlie's *ooge*," says John, delighted, as we all are, with any word we pick up from the Farmer. "He's as ooge as a house," says John, who once walked underneath him and out the other side like a doorway. And so he is huge; as huge as a tree, huger than a mountain, the hugest horse in all the world.

Today he came and watched us paddling up the green tunnel of the stream, as if we were exploring the Amazon, me in front with a stick to beat back the nettles, the children very cautiously behind.

"There might be snakes," said Peter, looking at my stick with approval, or crocodiles, I suppose, or lions and tigers (always together in our minds, though never in nature).

But we met nothing bigger than water-boatmen and minnows and, round a bend, the farm ducks absurdly upside down as they gobbled in the mud. Still we found a pool, deep enough for drowning if one really insisted on suicide, and the children are delighted. They have been back to look at it a dozen times since, jumping up from tea, squeezing like hens under the gate they cannot open, to gaze at the sinister dark water under the willows.

Here is magic and romance. They could *drown* in it. Die on their very doorstep. Their ordinary life has taken on suddenly a new depth and mystery, like finding in the kitchen cupboard a purple bottle labelled "poison," like holding death by the hand.

Of course they will never so much as dangle their toes in it again, for children, left to themselves, are the most careful of cowards. Only of traffic have they no proper instinctive fear, as if they were age-old animals who have learned to be frightened if they are to survive, but have not yet had time to develop the right ingrained reaction to this new danger of swiftly advancing motor-cars.

Of course one should say it in terms of mutations and natural selection, but still it would mean the same in the end. And however it happens, small children seem properly cautious of heights and poisons and death by drowning, of all the long-standing hazards.

"There's the Drowning Pool," they say, peering fascinated through the hedge. And half a field away, paddling on sand and pebbles in water which scarcely covers their feet, they pull each other back. "Don't go any further. It will drown you. It's *very* dangerous. Dardy, Dardy, come back! Dardy. Come back! You'll be *dead!*"

A Midsummer Night's Dream is an oddly inhuman play. It is not only the fairies who are kept so delicately outside our range of feeling, but even for the human beings our sympathies are never engaged. These troubled and despairing lovers are as much figures from a fairy-tale as the fairies themselves. Their transports are as formal and stylized, as far from human feeling, as ballet's passionless attitudes of love. Even poor Bottom and his friends, so anxious to please, so roughly mocked by the ungracious nobles, even they do not arouse our pity, but we laugh too. All is stylized, free of any burden of feeling, curiously remote. I wonder how many of our adult actions must seem like that to children, remote and meaningless formalities, quite without emotion.

Peter today fell and cut his knees, turning a delicate seasick green at the first sight of his own blood. It is odd that he should have grown so old without seeing it before, but neither of them seems to fall about to hurt himself. And it is one's own blood which matters, I find; other people's is simply the Midsummer Night's Dream. For they saw a pig killed and gutted in rivers of blood, watched with detached and quite unsqueamish interest, came back and told me the process in exact detail, with no emotion of any kind. Indeed I was the only one to be upset (besides, of course, the pig) that the children should be so exposed to horrors the moment I turned my back.

But I need not have worried, or at least I know too

little, even about the children I have lived with every day since they were born, to know when to worry. For the things we try to shield them from are not at all the things they mind. They seem to take the natural horrors for granted—killing and death—never having imagined, it seems, that the world was a gentle place. Yet they are overwhelmed by things we never thought to keep them from.

Unsuspecting, I took them by train to the seaside, and Peter sat quietly through the tedious journey, a very model of how the good child behaves in railway trains. But the night afterwards was a long, delirious horror. A dozen times he sprang up screaming, pointing wildly to the end of the bed as trains came thundering up, moaned and cowered in terror as they converged on him from all four walls of the bedroom. Such shrieks of dreadful nightmare that the skin still prickles down my spine to remember them.

Yet he was not asleep, he knew I was with him, there was no simple escape by waking. With a temperature of 103° there was no boundary between the real world and nightmare. There was nothing to do but talk to him about a new bird's nest I had found in the orchard, plan what we should do tomorrow, ask what he would like for lunch, and watch for his eyes to change from mad to sane, to focus on the real world which I saw too. But every so often he would listen again as he heard a phantom train come roaring up (it was the noise he seemed most to mind) and cling to me in agonizing terror.

Yet they fight their own demons, which is just as well, since we do not know how to help them. The next day Peter talked of trains with his usual affection, went to the station unconcerned, and was quite indifferent about his next journey. "I didn't like the train, but I don't mind now." Nor did he. The return journey was completely uneventful.

This morning John, too, came sobbing and frightened to find me making the beds.

JOHN: "I don't want to go and see Macaroni."

ME: "No, all right, you shan't. Who's Macaroni?"

JOHN: "She's a nasty little girl who lives in London. I don't like her."

ME: "Why not?"

JOHN: "She's got such *nasty* ears."

It is all quite serious, and he has no idea in the world that he made it all up himself, and has never even been to London.

Some time ago I bought a big old kitchen cupboard at a farmhouse sale, and ever since the children have so delighted to play house in it that the pans it was meant to hold are still getting dusty over the fireplace. They climb inside and pull the doors shut after them, John on the top shelf, Peter on the bottom. Then I must come along and knock. "Come in, come in," they call in muffled voices from top and bottom shelves, and I am to open the doors and greet them. Then we all go through the polite noises of someone meeting his neighbours, asking each other how we are, and talking about the weather. It is a set piece by now, and I am scornfully corrected whenever I try to skip because I am bored.

It seems an innocent game, but I shudder to think what the psychologists would make of it, this crouching in cupboards. But if the learned men no longer remember any normal childhood of their own, can they not at least *imagine* a child's delight in small things, a cupboard house its own size, in a world made to fit grown-ups, a world where everything is six times too large? If your nose just ledges on the table-top and a cup and saucer hides the cake behind as completely as Mount Everest, it really seems reasonable to use the underneath of the table for your tent, without having to drag in Freud. But the psychologists never seem to remember any of the ordinary days, only the bad moments.

Even the bad moments are not always what they imagine. One Summer day when I was a child, a naked man stepped out from the trees and stood in my path. It was surprising certainly, in a suburban park, but the fairy-tales were full of naked beggars wandering witless from their troubles, and that was what he looked like. Forlorn, unhappy, and cold. He was no more frightening than the other poor Tom who was a'cold on the heath, and no more concerned with me, except as an incidental audience.

He stood quite still with the trees behind him, and so did I, each looking at the other. Pitifully pinched and thin, he gazed out from his inner chaos through mild, wit-wandering eyes, his skin too white in the sunshine, and shadowed with green from the leaves.

We stared at each other for a long time, he looking always more ill and unhappy, I feeling more and more embarrassed. Not particularly because he had no clothes on —that only made it more obvious that he was mad—but because I, with all my wits, was self-conscious, and he, with only half his, was not. I could think of nothing to say to him to show I was sorry, without it also sounding rude, as from a child to a grown-up. I doubt whether I could think of anything to say even now, for there are some social situations one never gets enough practice with to become really urbane.

Then the police came. Well, the police, I knew (so long as I was not hanging on the back of lorries), were friendly, comfortable people. They would look after my poor man, and I could go on with my interrupted Summer morning and forget this adult problem which I did not know how to deal with.

But that was the bad moment. For the policemen grasped him roughly by his bony shoulders and pushed him stumbling in front of them. I would have liked to kill them. They were brutes! They were wicked! He was mad and unhappy. They must take care of him. He had done no harm. But I said not a word to help him, only stood by, a miserable self-conscious coward.

For a long time afterwards I was miserable and suspicious, avoiding everyone, and they thought they knew why. But what did I care whether poor mad Tom had any clothes on or not, when all the people I trusted, and thought I knew, might be blind and cruel inside like the policemen?

It has been an exhausting day of hacking back hedges, weeding, pruning, trying to bring the garden to some sort of order, to keep at bay the engulfing green.

Really I think I preferred the green wilderness as it was. It is not so much that I have made a desert and called it peace, but that more than all else I like old gardens run wild, urns half seen between unclipped trees, lilies struggling among the grass, old-fashioned roses tangled with brambles. One day I will make one on purpose, a deserted garden as the eighteenth century built deliberate ruins. For after all, one need only plant the lilies and roses, the grass and brambles will come of themselves. For that matter we are always here on the border of dereliction, we only have no urns to grace the tangle.

But gardens should only be neat if they are large, dark

cedars on lawns, and a village of glasshouses behind the mansion. And large gardens are easier to read about than to achieve.

Now for as much as *Gentlemen* are v. inquisitive, when were the best and securest Season for exposing their *Orange-trees* and more tender *Curiosities:* I give them this for a *Rule* the most infallible; that they observe the *Mulberry-tree* when it begins to put forth and open the leaves (be it earlier or later) bring your *Oranges* etc boldly out of the *Conservatory:* 'tis your only *season* to *transplant* and *Remove* them. Let this be done with care. If the tree be too ponderous to be lifted *perpendicular* by the Hand alone, by applying a *Triangle* and *Pulley*, and so with a *rope*, and a broad *Horse-girth* at the end, lapped about the Stem (to prevent galling) draw out the Tree with competent Mould adhering to it, having before loosend it from the sides of the *Case*, and so with ease transfer it to another. Then set your *Orange-trees* in the *shade* for a *Fortnight*, and afterwards expose them to the *Sun;* yet not where it is too searching by the reflection of *Walls*, but rather where they may have the gentle shade of distant *Trees*, or a *Palisade thin hedge*, or *Curtain* drawn before them, which may now and then be *sprinkled* with water, as *Seamen* do their Sails. The *morning Sun* till about *Three* in the Afternoon is best. Be not yet over-hasty in giving them the full *Sun*, for in your discreet acquainting than with this *change* consists their Prosperity during all the *Summer* after.

Dear John Evelyn and his *Gard'ner's Almanac*. How I would like him for neighbour, to call on him some sunny morning and find him gravely transplanting his *Orangetrees* with his home-made crane, like the pot-plants in the Luxembourg Gardens. And the orange trees themselves, such delicate, queenly creatures, living in pampered luxury, surrounded by curtains even, like leading ladies. I can only sigh with envy that their life should be so much Mary's and mine almost completely Martha's.

Still I have been taking stock ruthlessly, as one does now and again, and I find that I work much harder than I need, which is stupid. There is a smug, poverty-stricken school of morality which considers things like hard work and getting up early in the morning as virtuous in themselves. But what nonsense. It is only inefficient not to arrange one's affairs to have time for a civilized life.

"Mere living wears the most of life away." Yes, it does. Especially in war-time. But if mere living is to wear away the *whole* of life, then the living itself becomes pointless, like cooking and cooking meals which never get eaten.

So I have divided my activities into three. Essential, Martha, and Mary.

The essential is really surprisingly small; it is only that it must be done always, rain or shine. The children must be loved, fed, and disciplined (though I am not at all sure that the discipline should not come before the affection, and certainly before the food). Then the house must be kept clean and tidy, since I am only good-tempered in a peaceful house, and I must read to keep us all sane.

Martha's tedious activities, when looked at closely, are mostly to satisfy the grown-ups' sense of propriety, and not at all for the benefit of the children. Are mostly fuss. It is pleasant, of course, to have shoes cleaned, and sheets ironed, and a tablecloth for meals, but really it makes no difference to anyone in the end. The children care not a scrap, and neither, when I look hard, do I. Not if I must pay for such superficialities with the precious little time left over from essentials. Clean pyjamas are just as comfortable for a bed-time story whether ironed or not, and if they are to be ironed, then there is no time left for *Peter Rabbit*.

I suppose it must be better to have cooked meals instead of living on milk as we mostly do, and perhaps it is worth trailing off to dull indoor tea-parties to let the children practise their manners, but perhaps not. Certainly it does not matter that the children are dirty and untidy most of the time, for they are so in any case, by an unalterable natural law.

So from now on I shall allow Martha just so much time, and if the socks are not darned at the end, then we will all go on wearing the holes. For the children will remember a hundred things of their childhood, but not whether their clothes were mended, and neither, in ten years' time, shall I.

And we shall all remember the Mary parts, the geraniums on the kitchen windowsill. Yet Mary, oddly, is the difficult one. It is easy to plod on conscientiously, washing six sheets every Monday simply because Monday is washday, but hard to say firmly: "No. The sheets can wait. Every Monday every week can be wash-day, but only once or twice a year this perfect blue weather and the fields white over with dog-daisies. So today we will go and sit in them, and do no work at all."

It would be simpler, of course, if the sheets were not waiting there the next day. Still not really simple, for it is always easier, it seems, to be virtuous than charming. But I try: I brush my hair, and put on a clean frock, and say: "Now I am Mary." But it needs practice. Every so often Martha gives an irresistible nudge, and beyond a certain stage of muddiness I cannot help myself reminding the children to change their shoes.

TODAY we visited a friend in the local hospital, and the children took a cottagey bunch of flowers they had picked themselves from the garden, for the right to give presents is a delicate privilege which we should not take for granted even with the sick. There are few people any of us would choose to be grateful to, gratitude being a difficult emotion in all kinds of ways, and except towards those we are fond of, an imposed indignity.

Understanding, above all, is a gift we should never offer uninvited. We each preserve our poor self-respect behind a façade of reticence and restraint, and unsought sympathy from an indifferent world is an unbearable intrusion. Even from our friends it is an embarrassment, and from our enemies a personal insult. It is only from those we love and completely trust that we welcome understanding, and even from them it may easily become unendurable, an intrusion on our privacy. Even the loved ones should only look in on our inmost self by invitation. And the easiest comfort of all to accept is that which we feel to be offered unconsciously, by happy chance and not by understanding: the post which brings a delightful invitation on the morning of our melancholy.

The children were enthralled by the new world of the hospital ward, staring in amazement at so many grownups in bed in the middle of the day. "Are they very tired?" they asked. "Do they have to rest like we do?"

And because always, if one has a dog or a small child, one becomes somehow a public figure, and because everyone feels he can talk to you thus accompanied, without further introduction, we must stop to talk a little at every bed.

Despite all my resolutions I was appalled by the ennui of hospital afternoons, of hospital tea on the veranda, coarse grass with cigarette-ends and bits of bandage, the Gramophone next door, and the desultory small-talk of always the same people. An arid texture, like shop cakes gone stale.

But no one seemed to mind. It feels, I suppose, quite different as a life lived from the inside, has its own coherence and significance, so that my sympathy is not only tactless but ridiculous.

Peter is fascinated now by hospitals. He calls them hoffys.

"Where's the kitchen in that big hoffy?"

"In the middle."

"No. I think it's at the end. That's a bedroom in the middle. What's that big house for?"

"That's another hospital."

"No. Hoffys don't have chimneys. Hoffys don't have curtains."

Perhaps after all he is not so unobservant as I think, but only illogical.

"I like those warbler-trees," he said, looking at a row of Lombardy poplars on the road back. I asked why he called them that. "Because they're so wriggly," he said. This is too esoteric for me, for I am sure he does not know what warble means. But "bean-trees" for laburnums is easy enough, and "worm-fishing" quite exactly describes the thrushes looking for worms on the lawn.

Sometimes I get them both to define simple words, to amuse myself at the difference in their minds.

ME: "What is a house?" (They are always anxious to play, for it is exhausting how much children enjoy educational games.)

PETER: "A house is a big thing with chimneys and windows, where you keep tables and logs. Spiders live in it."

But John says simply and firmly: "A house is made of walls and built with bricks."

ME: "What is a motor-car?"

PETER (for it must always be Peter who answers first, as John's logical version overwhelms his own impressionistic one, and he says only: "Yes, that's what it is. Yes"):

"A motor-car is something with a lot of windows and four wheels, and everything outside it spins."

Well I know about the spinning, it is my favourite game in trains. Trees and houses near the railway-line spin round as we rush by seeing them first from one side, then the other. And things in the distance, a hill or the sailing moon, keep pace with us, seem to travel forward at the same speed as the train. But a motor-car, says John, "runs along the road for people to ride in."

Still John too can talk nonsense enough when he wants to. "Now it's a church with a weather-cock on top," he says, taking a bite from his biscuit. Then another mouthful: "Now it's higgledy-piggledy my black hen. Only it's brown. Now it's like the moon when it's thin."

IF you turn turn down the lane away from the village, follow the windings for half a mile or so between the tall elms, you come to our toy railway. Not the real one with a station and trains going to London, but a single line across the meadows, with gates for it to cross every lane it meets. And the games for this railway are quite different from those for the real station. Here we put halfpennies on the rails and hope to find them flattened to pennies by the passing train. But we never do find them, neither as pennies or halfpennies—never find them at all.

We have competitions (written with a stick in the dust at the edge of the road because the children cheat) to guess whether, when the train comes, the engine will be running backwards or forwards, how many coaches there will be, and how many passengers. One passenger it is mostly, for we can see right through the windows to the sky at the other side, one coach, and the engine going backwards.

Then there are the gates to climb on, to swing on as they open, the engine-driver to wave to, and for me, early purple orchises among the cowslips in the next-door meadow, and whinchats in Summer balancing on the telegraph wires. Then as the train comes thundering past, we lie against the embankment for the terrified pleasure of feeling the solid ground shake beneath us like an earthquake.

And sometimes there is the wife of the man who opens the gates for the trains, and we talk about London. She came out here, months ago now, a homesick Cockney, bringing her two children when their house was bombed. And here she has stayed ever since, not a jot less homesick, but resolved to put up with her exile because her husband is proud of his garden, and her children thrive on country air.

She is always dressed pathetically for a jaunt, with a gay ribbon in her curled yellow hair, and pink pearl earrings. And not a soul to notice in these lonely fields but the cows staring vaguely over the hedge.

"That's my room," she says, pointing to a little window over the front door. "I like to look over the street." And she smiles at the distant hills, across the blowy, empty country where the yellow-hammers sing, seeing the cheerful London traffic, and friends gossiping, and the cinema on the corner.

Nothing one can do to a fish in its river is as dreadful as simply lifting it out of the water, and she is one of the real heroines.

"THEY shoot up like young willows," the Farmer said, looking at the unsuitable length of leg now left uncovered by Peter's trousers. And I suppose they do. Certainly they do, for all their sleeves are retreating gradually to their elbows. But still they are always much smaller than I expect. I never go to London without being astonished when I come back that they still cannot reach the latch on the kitchen door.

The latch, for all the kitchen end of the house has latches instead of door-knobs, giving a delightful feeling of living half out-of-doors. Perhaps all old houses feel the same, or perhaps it is because when we came to this one it had been empty for fifteen years and become part of the orchard. Weeds grew round the kitchen, nettles and groundsel in the leaves drifted down the wide open chimney, and an elm tree struggled through a crack in the floor. Ivy had crept in at the windows, and the orchard grown so high all around that the only light in the ground-floor rooms was a filtered green gloom like the bottom of a pool. Robins lived here when we came, and have tried to ever since, flying in whenever the windows are open, though I chase them out always for the mess they make. And we could stand in the fireplaces and look at the sky up the chimney, though not see stars at midday as they told me as a child I should from the bottom of a well.

Even now that we have put chimney-pots on the chimneys and weeded the kitchen floor, we are never properly indoors, for the brick walls and tiled floors, and beams still shaped like the trees they once were, belong more to the outside of a house than the inside.

Besides, it is not only the robins, though they still fly constantly from one door to the other. But an owl came in one night and perched enormous till morning on a ledge in Peter's bedroom, sinister and predatory. One hard Winter we found a dead kestrel in the smoky kitchen flue, and last night a bat came in at my window, fluttering endlessly at bewildering speed in the containing walls, until it crouched at last exhausted in a corner, with enormous ears like a ram's horns, like shells, as if it were listening to the sea. But still the small, frightened creature looked quite astonishingly evil, as if it *must* bite or sting, or spit out poison, like the horrible creatures of Hieronymus Bosch's nightmares.

At the first spell of bad weather, mice from the garden come in and live with us under cover, and in Autumn great spiders suspended on their crooked legs. Ivy and jasmine still grow in at the windows set open for the Summer, and in Winter dozens of butterflies hibernate with us, small tortoise-shells and peacocks, clinging to the rough beams in odd corners. All Winter I am not allowed to open the windows on windy days for fear our visitors blow away, and the children play at breathing on them to make them come alive, flapping their wings (rather dusty the colours are by Spring) in a dazed, half-hearted way. Thank goodness John does not seem to consider they need taming.

Under the overhanging eaves of the house there are long tunnels between the rafters of the roof, and here the starlings nest as their right, a determined small flock of them, driving away the hopeful sparrows. They were here, I suppose, before we came, like all the rest, but that did not stop me, when we first arrived, from trying to limit them to reasonable numbers. I rolled newspaper into balls and stuffed it into the holes, but the next morning the lawn was white with torn shreds, and the starlings home again. I put bricks in the holes, and the birds squeezed by. I tried netting, and they found gaps. For they were more determined than I was, and after such an intimate battle of wits I had grown fond of them.

Of course they are a nuisance. They begin to carry in straw for their nests any mild days after Christmas, and being the untidiest of birds, the garden soon comes to look like the rick-yard. All through nesting-time the windows are streaked with white droppings, as if we were endlessly spring-cleaning, and the restless nights of early Summer are disturbed by the cheeping and scuffling of their noisy broods above our heads.

But there are compensations. Starlings make pleasantly clownish companions, and one soon gets to know the individual birds—one has a white wing feather, one a short tail, one a long beak, one a voice lower even than the rest. Their tuneless, gurgling song has its own charm, and they are brilliant mimics. One, especially, so exactly copies the cowman's whistle that I often look for the man in astonishment on the chimney-top.

In Winter they sun themselves with the sparrows on the south slopes of our hilly roof, and perch in rows of crochets along every ridge of the tiles, turning the house to fairy-tale. In Spring they decorate the entrance to their nests with arabis and heads of primroses, a pretty anthropomorphic fancy. They are always noisy, especially the young, who come from the nest to the edge of the eaves and squawk with impatience for the caterpillar they know is coming. For the parents bring food at almost exactly regular intervals, carrying away the droppings on the outward flight to a quite pernickety distance.

When the young leave the nest they stay about the farm for a time, the greyish young in one flock, the tired parents in another. But after a week or two they all disappear, and we are quiet until Autumn. Then they come back, the regular well-known inhabitants, without their young, but with new tricks. One of them can call exactly like a sea gull's cry, and I like to think they have all been away for a well-earned seaside holiday without their children, feeding (for themselves now) on the mud of estuaries, with their unexpected slow walk (they must be the smallest birds to walk and not hop or run) which makes them look, in feeding flocks, more like animals than birds.

THIS Sunday afternoon I sat in the sun against the wall of the house and listened to the Beethoven concert through the open window. But even the *Pastoral Symphony* will not do out-of-doors; it is not tawdry exactly, but somehow like wearing evening dress in daytime, or coming out of theatre matinées into sunny streets. The different worlds simply will not mix, and in the encounter it is always the world man has made which is cheapened. I often wonder just how awful Proust's concerts must have sounded on Balbec beach, with the enormous sea for background, and the sharp voices of children.

But in August I long for the sea, such a dull and inelegant month it is here: grow restless to escape from this leafy, shut-in Summer to the huge, clean, empty sea.

It is the light, above all, that is different at the sea. Not only that the sun, direct or diffused, shines from a wider arch of sky where there are no trees or hills to close in the horizon, but that the surfaces it shines on are different, the brilliant sea and sand, and the land bleached with sun and salt winds. So that the light does not simply shine down from the sky as it does here, but is reflected, a ubiquitous quality of the air. People's faces are lit unexpectedly from below, with a pearly sheen where one expects shadows, pale under their chins and eyebrows. The outlines too of figures are different, edged with dark instead of light against the brilliance, like Stubbs's most magical paintings. And the figures themselves are the only dark and solid objects in the shimmering seascape, like a Boudin picture. Strangely symbolic they are, figures by the sea. Not only against the enhancing shore background, but even walking home barefoot in family parties from the beach, with all the innocent bright paraphernalia of a day's picnicking. They seem, not Mr. and Mrs. Brown with their half-grown children, but the very symbol of the human family on holiday.

Then there is the noise of a beach. For on the stillest day one is conscious always of an unheard roar, as if so great a volume of air reverberated of itself, though on a note outside our range of hearing. And the steady rattling of the sea, like paper crumpled a long way off, and distant voices as high and shrill as the gulls themselves.

I am homesick always in August for the pleasures of lost holidays, the smell of rubber raincoats and bathing-caps, sand grating in the lids of sandwich tins and the tops of thermos-flasks, and treasured for months after, loose in the bottoms of pockets and in the toes of shoes, a magic dust from the other, the holiday world. There was the smell of seaweed in the sun, like an overripe Camembert cheese, and clean, smooth-worn pebbles and shells, and the way one's hands got white from the salt, between the fingers and round the nails.

I want to wake up, not in this bowery leafiness to a working-day, but with the sea-blink shining on the ceiling, like the light from snow but softer, and the day's business only to arrange when we shall bathe because of the tide, the lovely uneven tide which banishes monotony in the most uneventful of holidays. I want the buffety weather on the cliff-tops, then the delicious relief of shutting oneself in the sheltered house, away from the wind which one comes to hate like a cat.

It is not homesickness for the sea, since I fear the sea and never feel at home there, but holiday-sickness. The sea, for landlubbers, is only to visit. I can never forget the dreadful boom it makes in storms, a terrifying dull thud, so that even in the bluest Summer calm it is like living with a capricious monster which only by chance does not destroy us all.

But holidays are difficult now, as they never were when one was twelve or so. Not more difficult to achieve, for that is only an accident of war-time, but more difficult to enjoy. Real holidays, I mean, not simply recovering from exhaustion, or baby-minding by the sea instead of at home. Real holidays, going to places because one wants to see them.

For then we take ourselves about, our minds and senses, our memories and emotions, take them travelling about and expose them to new impressions and experiences. And for a time—it depends how eager we are, how untired when we started—we react intensely to the stimulus. To the new country, the different inflections of the voices, the changed architecture, the subtly different ways of living everyday life. Even the smell of the strange water, the texture of foreign bread under our fingers. We live each day, however uneventful, at a high pitch of feeling and thinking, we are twice as alive as usual.

But not for long. We cannot long react so acutely for twenty-four hours of every day, for even the noises outside our window while we sleep are new and strange, they must be accepted by our unconscious ears unless we are to wake up at every sound. So that quite quickly our responses flag, like a muscle overstimulated and exhausted. Very soon we feel nothing at all when faced with new wonders, we might as well read the guidebook and look at the photographs, for we can do nothing for ourselves.

This stage of the holiday is critical, we are in danger of

a mood which Pater says is "known to all passably sentimental wayfarers as night deepens again and again over
their path, in which all journeying, from the known to
the unknown, comes suddenly to figure as a mere foolish
truancy—like a child's running away from home—with
the feeling that one had best return at once, even through
the darkness."

It is not only homesickness we suffer, but also boredom, boredom surely being the arch-enemy which waits
in ambush for all travellers. One is homeless in hotels, or
moving from place to place; and because, away from
home and one's own small daily affairs, there is nothing
to fill the odd hours—the hour waiting for dinner, the
hour recovering from a morning's sight-seeing—nothing
to fill them but the aimless time-killing of public rooms,
the days can seem interminably long. An hour which
leaks away from the busy day at home while we simply
walk round the garden, seems in the sitting-room of a
hotel an eternity of boredom.

We lose the habit of being transplanted, like a tree un-
disturbed growing roots into a settled life. The days on
holiday have no further significance, no part in the rest
of our lives, but must each be lived for itself, must be its
own reward. They are not carried along by the rhythm
of our coherent existence as ordinary days are, but must
each exist as separate and complete occasions which may
or may not succeed. Sometimes indeed they do succeed
superbly, stay with us always as perfect and unassailable
memories. But not often. Not often enough. Too often
we only remember how dusty the roads were, how weary
we were in the last museum, how we could not sleep because of the singing in the street. For though the first delighted response to strangeness passes, we are still left
hypersensitive to irritations, like skin after fever. Perhaps

one should take constant sedatives on holiday, after the first few rapturous days. And certainly at the end. On the last day we are faced with nothing but the tiresomeness of packing and getting ourselves home again, the tedium of the journey back. I never go to bed on the last night without feeling that I would willingly sacrifice all future holidays only to wake up the next morning at home, without the journey. A ruthless impatience to be back, as if our accustomed life were a magnet which increases in strength as we get nearer, a solid body of living which draws us by its own gravitational power. To turn aside on the way home has always been an impossible frustration. For we can travel happily and indefinitely forward, exploring new country, putting every day a greater distance between ourself and setting out, but let us once turn back towards the magnet and the pull begins. We must go home fast and straight, like a horse to its stable, travelling day and night if need be.

Even Horace Walpole, the most sophisticated of travellers, felt the same. "I have so absolutely lost all curiosity, that, except the towns in the straight road to Great Britain, I shall scarce see a jot more of a foreign land."

There was never this trouble with childhood seaside holidays. At that age a fortnight was a lifetime, and quite simply one settled into a new life, wherever it was, arranging shells along the mantelpiece, keeping a special blue pebble under the pillow, knowing spades and buckets were always in the same corner of the porch, and which shop was best for ice cream. By the end of the first day one knew every landmark on the way down to the beach, every pool on the shore and flower on the cliffs. One was not a stranger, but at home, and living one's proper life. The days were not disconnected, but made a coherent pattern. Today we must bring up extra sea-water for the crabs and starfish in the bucket in the garden, because tomorrow we were going off for the whole day to a new bay beyond the point. Next week we must bathe in the mornings and go exploring in the afternoons, because high tide is at tea-time and the beach covered.

That is how they used to take their holidays. Where we rush down for a week-end and are bored, they settled in for a month and were not. For it is moving fast which bores us, not moving slowly. Aeroplanes, not walking. We need time to grow roots to live by. So Henry James's people took a house in Venice, a suite in Paris, and lived their time there, settling in and evolving an ordered daily round.

So one Summer I will find a house by the sea and live there with the children, but now we can only go our Summer picnics in the hills, pretending that the steep escarpment is cliffs above the green sea of the Vale. And on our last picnic I enjoyed what has become, in these days of no cameras, a too rare pleasure. I watched a young couple take each other's photographs; shy but confident figures silhouetted against the infinite view. It is a good game always, but best of all in Paris, a perfect occupation for sunny mornings when really, from visual indigestion, one cannot sight-see any longer. Not even the Place des Vosges, nor the Île Saint-Louis, nor even the enchanting bird-market on Sunday morning.

First the photographers choose their background, the Louvre, the Arc de Triomphe, or (the greatest favourite of all) the fountain in the Place de la Concorde. For nothing, it seems, overawes them, not the Champs Elysées, not the Sphinx, not the Acropolis itself.

When they have chosen the background—two birds with one stone, I suppose they feel—then they pose.

Awkwardly, self-consciously, and always with the sun full in their eyes. First she (for the order never varies), the girl smiling sideways because of the sun, not knowing what to do with her hands. Then he, the young man, with his hands behind him, and throwing out his chest till it stretches the buttons on the coat he has carefully fastened.

"There," they will say to half-bored, half-envious audiences when they get back home. "There. That's Amy," hiding the vista of the Champs Elysées, but they do not say so. "And that's me," half blown away on the Eiffel Tower, an outsize mechanical monstrosity which I think the French must simply be forgiven for liking, as we must be forgiven the Albert Memorial.

WE need some way of experiencing large surfaces besides just looking at them. I know the curve of our hills by heart, but it is not enough. I need some other way of making contact with them. Cycling over them will not do, switch-backing over the dips and rises, for they are too large. It needs a giant's size to feel the gentle tops under your hand, to run your thumb along the shallow valleys, to stroke the fields of long grass, and ruffle the tops of the leafy woods.

Still there is nothing so good for reviving a view one has grown too used to by the end of Summer, for seeing it new and vivid again, nothing so good as looking at it upside down. The children bend over and peer between their legs, but it is less undignified to lie flat and look backwards. Perhaps the National Gallery should hang its pictures upside down from time to time, so that we look at them afresh, see the real balance of the patterns we have grown too used to.

There are other ways, without standing on one's head,

of seeing things vividly. One can lie in the grass with a mind completely blank. "I am new-born," one can say. "When I open my eyes, I shall see for the very first time. And what I see will have no meaning, no explanation, no relevance to anything I know, for I know nothing. I shall see it, not with my mind, but directly for itself. The first sound I hear I shall hear for the very first time, it will have no meaning beyond its own vibration. The feel of the wind, the smell of the grass, are strange sensations I have never felt before."

It gives the scene a vivid immediacy. The trees, above all, are astonishing presences, immense, swaying as if they were alive, with a metallic rustle of leaves in high Summer, and mysteriously from their leafiness come the strange, high calls of unseen, unimaginable birds.

So I amuse myself as the children do, out here in the orchard, for we are all becalmed and happy in the rich boredom of late Summer, all true content being partly a happy boredom.

Day after day of settled sunshine, with the flowers over and the birds finished nesting, finished singing almost, for August is a quiet month in the country, and the starlings have left us. Scattered hens peck among the hay-stubble, the cows swish resignedly at the accustomed flies, and the children make long-term plans for damming the stream, for building a house in the great willow tree, as if their year should be an endless Summer day.

This is the time of all the year when being a human is the most peaceful. The restlessness and dissatisfaction are quiet, our over-sensitive responses slowed down, and Keats's "wakeful anguish of the soul" is only an unreal memory from the dark Winter. Our minds cease to drive us, these endless days of sunshine, and we can recover in simple animal content.

I watch for an hour together a beetle moving through its green-lit world beneath a roof of nettles, passing easily from my own life to the insect's, seeing myself reflected in this other world, a strange and gaudy mountain.

Or even that becomes too strenuous an occupation, and I lie in the sun and do nothing whatsoever, seeing only the piled majestic clouds sail from one horizon to the other, hearing the children's voices a long way off, the rattle of the reaper and binder over the corn. The creeper and binder, John calls it, "because it creeps along and binds the corn into bunches."

Even our bodies share this shielding of the spirit by mindless well-being. We take on a fine layer of fat just beneath the skin, insulating our nerves from shock as a seal's fat saves him from the cold. And over the smooth fat our skin becomes taut and glossy, like the coats of the plump young calves in the meadow. If we bit our arms, the skin would snap like the skin of an apple, and the blood come beading out like juice. Even the movements of our bodies change, smoothing out the fidgeting and jerkiness to simple gestures.

When a ball is thrown into the air, there is a moment of poised stillness before it falls again. Late Summer is this same moment between growing and dying, it has a tranced, timeless quality which could go on for eternity like the nights of midwinter. It is the least urgent of all the seasons. And in this sunshine which will last for ever, we can at last live like those who are born wise, can live in the present moment as if we had that alone to live, without past or future. It is only on rare and happy occasions that we can escape from the whole pattern of our lives. The moment almost never exists for itself, but is given its meaning from all that will follow or went before. Almost never do we ask: "Is this a perfect afternoon with this person I may never meet again?" But trouble ourselves to know whether this is a friend for always, a new colour changing the whole pattern, and all the wavy lines a little altered. Feeling still, as the children do, even though I no longer believe it, that we can take hands and promise to be friends for ever.

So that always there are echoes from before and after over everything one does. But not today in this changeless Summer. Today between its two nights is an occasion without reference, is perfect and complete. For this Summer we walk, all three of us, on hills we shall never find again.

PART FOUR

AUTUMN

TO GO BLACKBERRYING ON A FINE AU-
tumn day is the most comprehensive of pleasures.
First there is the weather, blue and gold where Spring,
when the light should be the same, is blue and silver. The
sky is a high milky azure (that favourite colour of French
poets), fading to grey at the horizon, and though the sun
is still warm, the air already has a cool sharpness in the
shadows. The trees are changing colour, their branches of
fading leaves drooping as gracefully and artificially as
sprays arranged in a florist's window, a fleeting fragile
beauty without purpose or urgency. It is a tranquil pleasure, the Autumn weather, with little of Spring's restless
dissatisfaction, for Autumn is the most civilized of seasons, the furthest from the animal state, as the middle-
aged are a product of the culture they live in, but the
young are driven by universal and primitive dreams. So
Autumn is civilized where Spring is savage, the easiest
of the seasons to live with.

· 177 ·

Then all the paraphernalia of blackberrying is pleasant. One's oldest and friendliest clothes, thermos-flasks and picnic lunch, and wicker baskets for the dark, shining fruit and occasional mushrooms. The dog too, who chases zigzag across the fields, her coat renewed and glossy after the Summer moult, nose down and tail flying, scattering the whirring partridges. And the children are delightful company, their high spirits, so oppressive in the house, evaporated harmlessly in the open air. Even half a dozen of them together—for blackberrying should always be a party, the easiest of all ways of returning hospitality.

Each child has his own mug or tin auxiliary to the main baskets, but after the first ten minutes children are more decorative than useful as blackberry-pickers, even though one leaves for them all the lower branches. They eat too many, their mouths tell-tale with purple moustaches; and it is odd, this messiness with blackberries, for all other food has gone unerringly into their mouths since infancy.

The older children can be bribed to go on picking with promises of their own jars of jam to arrange for themselves in rows on the pantry shelf. They write their own labels, beginning with strange spelling variations of "Blackberry and Apple" but soon, succinctly, "B & A."

But the younger ones care nothing for future pleasures. They fill their mugs with hips and haws and thistledown, and spread a few deceiving blackberries like cream on the top. This practical joke they then offer to the grown-ups in explosive merriment, and each time one must pretend to be taken in, though they know as well as I do that my surprise is deliberate pantomime. Still I must exclaim at the trick with mock rage, and chase and roll them in the short, lush grass which has grown through the hay-stubble with the Autumn rains and holds the dew till midday.

It is surprising that blackberries flower so late, not till

July and August, though they are to ripen before the Winter. There must too be different sub-species of brambles, those furthest north ripening first, not because the northern Summer is earlier, but because the Winter is. For I remember we always found them ripe in the August holidays on the Yorkshire coast.

There are other minor pleasures on these blackberrying picnics. One takes just enough exercise, but not enough to be tired, and since we need go no further than a field away from the house, there is no trailing back with tired children at the end of the day. And if the baskets are heavy to carry, it is a satisfactory weight, a hoard of treasure won for the Winter.

Then there is the ruthless pleasure of tearing old clothes free from clinging branches, and in the bath at night, the rash of scratches which prick and smart in the hot water. For this too is part of the day's enjoyment, as the slight sharpness is part of the flavour of a Cox's orange pippin. And in bed at last, under closed eyelids, there is still a pattern of bramble leaves and tangled flowers and shining purple berries, a print on our eyes which has not yet faded from the long day in the hedges, as the sun when we have looked at it leaves swimming coloured balls on the empty air.

One can imagine a sensibility so subtle and over-wrought that to go blackberrying might satisfy the whole range of human feeling. We think of Virginia Woolf and of Mrs. Dalloway walking out to buy flowers for her party. And indeed Virginia Woolf is the perfect bedside book for visitors who come to stay with us here, for we live in the right receptive quiet.

Yet I am never quite happy reading her; there is always a vague underlying sadness. Perhaps it is the feeling that a mind as sensitive as hers can never long survive our world of crude and violent shocks. So that as she watches each ripple of her conciousness, catches and pins it as surely and delicately as a butterfly, we are afraid always that she will lose her balance, that she will so refine and make sensitive the instrument of her mind that it must inevitably be destroyed.

But then, too, there was once a young man who told me that his heart missed a beat only to see her name on the dust-jacket of a book. Virginia Woolf. It is the only time I have ever been jealous. But I suffered then—long ago it seems now—such an agonizing wave of misery, such an inmost stab of pain, that I have never read her since without a faint echo of uneasiness.

TODAY down the lane we watched a man ploughing a field in a swirl of seagulls. And thinking how Jean-Jacques Rousseau would have approved, I told the children about parallel lines as they watched the turning furrows.

I am astonished every time at how much faster a child's brain develops than its emotional life. For emotionally these two are still as inhuman and uncontrolled as animals, dominated by every irrational mood and fancy, utterly unconcerned with any reactions but their own. Yet they understand abstract ideas quickly and easily, parallel lines and evolution, asking always for more. It is as if the brain, being man's speciality, lived its own detached life independent of the struggling emotions which must re-create painfully his long history of development.

Walking down the lane opposite the escarpment of the hills, the accustomed landscape is new and different in the afternoon sun. For there is a curious sideways slant of the light in Autumn which gives a new quality to the familiar view. The curves and hollows of the hills are changed, the shadows of trees are a field long over the stubble, and haystacks are lit unexpectedly from the side. Sometimes at evening the sunny land is lighter than the darkening east, giving a strange effect of storm, though the air is serene and clear.

This is the end of September, three months from the Summer Equinox. So that at the end of March the light should be the same. But I never remember it so. Spring light has never this lingering caressing quality, is never mellow and irradiating like this. But next March I shall remember and watch. The hills will still be there, even if the trees have no leaves to make shadows, and though the haystacks are eaten for Winter feed.

Haystacks are surely the most satisfactory shape that man has ever created. When serious people talk about Significant Form, I think of haystacks. The round ones with their thatched tops gathered to a single point. There is only one old man left in these parts, the Farmer says, who can still thatch them so that they keep out the wet, and no one left at all who can make straw dollies to put on the top.

Seen in two dimensions, flat, they are five-sided, as if the points of a star had been joined to make it comfortable. But superimposed on their five-sidedness is the circle of their round roof and cone-shaped sides (for they are *built* narrower at the bottom, it is not only that the animals get in and nibble away the foundations as I used to think). In outline the curves do not show, only the five straight sides, but the edge of the thatch sweeps from corner to corner in an ellipse which we continue mentally round the other side, and the sunshine edges round their curved walls, picking out odd straws against the shadow. So that looking at them, one sees both the joined star and the plan of concentric circles, an intellectual conception

as satisfying as one's first school geometry. Yet a haystack
is not a dead and perfect shape of the geometry book, but
a human creation, with the slight irregularities of all
things which have grown or are hand-made, making them
always more intimate and personal than machine perfection. I think somewhere there must be a fairy-tale of
someone who fell in love with a haystack.

It is an Autumn of tranquil sun, but ominous with the
threat of Winter advancing like a northern enemy. The
farm is busy storing grain and beans and turnips, coal and
logs, against the cold and dark. The Summer birds have
escaped, the Winter regulars grown plump with new
feathers, and soon now the trees will shrink back into the
hard wood, shedding their vulnerable leaves,

> *Quite underground, as flowers depart*
> *To feed their mother-root when they have*
> *blown;*
> *Where they together*
> *All the hard weather*
> *Dead to the world, keep house unknown.*

I still take the children to the station for their Friday
trains, but troubled now by an echo of Spring's restless
need to break away.

"Look at the fading, many-coloured woods"—it is
from Thomson's *Seasons*, I think, but I am tired of the
country. Of course it has never looked lovelier, but I am
tired of exclaiming, even to myself. The charm of the
simple life palls by the end of Summer, and I long for
London. Here there is tea round the nursery fire, there
the urgent trains roaring through the dusk to the great
city. And which do I want?

Five years ago I should never have imagined the nursery tea-party could be anything but a task, another five

years and perhaps the lighted cities will have lost their fascination. But now among these dim, wet fields I suffer growing-pains as acute as any adolescent. And indeed of my own adolescence the only growing-pains I remember are a long and desperate boredom.

Our troubles are hardest to cure, hardest to bear even, when they are intangible. Restlessness, dissatisfaction, they are subtler enemies than the real griefs, for they are not accidents from outside ourselves which still leave us intact to suffer them, but contagions spreading from our inner spirit to poison our whole world. My boredom was a desperate malady:

> *Rien n'égale en longueur les boiteuses journées*
> *Quand sous les lourds flocons des neigeuses*
> *années*
> *L'Ennui, fruit de la morne incuriosité*
> *Prend les proportions de l'immortalité.*

Well, it was not for me born of incuriosity, but of some adolescent fever. But certainly it seemed immortal, the one reality. The world at fourteen or so was stale, "weary, stale, flat and unprofitable." Nothing that could ever happen to me, I felt, could seem significant, could engross me, could dispel this mood of miserable indifference. And by its very nature, the boredom lengthened every day, every minute, into eternity. One might be sad for an hour, and the hour seem long, but to be bored for five minutes was to be bored for the whole of one's life.

Enhancing the weariness, I suffered too from an all-embracing disgust at the dirt and ugliness and squalor of the poor industrial town where I lived. Being young, I had no pity for this wretchedness, but only hate—I hated it all, the poor shoddy houses, the derelict spaces between

them, the uncleared litter in the streets, the stunted people who talked in their throats instead of their mouths,
the clanging trams, the gaudy shops, the harsh factories
which dominated the town's life like preying monsters.
Twenty-seven factory chimneys I could count from my
schoolroom window, and there would have been more
still if the smoke from the twenty-seven had not blotted
out the rest.

Above all, I hated the dirt, hated the film of soot and
oil and grit which blackened every building, fouled the
country for miles around, and killed the pansies I could
never coax to grow in my square of sooty garden. Coming back in the train from clean seaside holidays to this
detested filth, I would comfort myself with wild plans of
digging a channel to bring the great salty sea rollicking in
and wash the city clean like the Augean stables. Leaving,
instead of dirty tram-tickets and fish-and-chip papers,
silver sand in the gutters, and the white pavement scattered with starfish and pale, fragile shells.

Hatred involves us as closely as love with the object
which stirs us, and I bitterly resented this City of Dreadful Night which obsessed my mind. And because hatred
creates nothing, because it destroys us, I suffered a desperate expense of spirit. For our emotions are not simple.
We feel the emotion itself, but also the mind's reaction to
it, as, for instance, we are ashamed of being a coward, or
embarrassed at crying in public.

But we are all in some way unhappy, it seems, during
our adolescence, and the boredom and the town were my
miseries, leaving scars which trouble me still whenever I
hear church bells. It seems an odd association, and took
me as long to trace as the Madeleines took Proust, but all
through my school-days we lived in a house near a
church. And the bells would ring and ring through the

endless Sundays when I longed for the country, so un-
attainably far away in that huge, sprawling city.

So that church bells ringing still bring back the boredom of those unhappy days, even here, blowing loud or
soft in the wind across the fields and hedges from the
village church. Yet these are endearing bells, rung by the
vicar and the doctor and enthusiastic villagers, rung badly
and earnestly, with hesitations and sudden rushes, as if
the bells themselves had a stammer. I tell myself they are
charming; how country people have always loved bells
across meadows; I think of Christmas cards.

But it is no use. At the first hesitant tumble of sound
in the wind, a blight of boredom descends on the green
fields, and I am oppressed again by the old weariness of
spirit unknown since adolescence.

THE weather has changed to a cold and sullen stillness,
and this has been the day which comes every Autumn,
when all hope dies. The hills are lost in a cold half-mist,
the fields flat and dead in the grey light, and the Winter
stretches ahead endlessly to a Spring we cannot even try
to believe in. After the long days of sunshine we realize
again suddenly that the Winter is dark. Cold, too, and
shut in and melancholy, but, above all, dark, with the
short hours of grudging daylight only an interruption of
the settled night.

It is absurd at this grown-up age to be still afraid of the
dark, but all the reasoning in the world makes no difference. There are days when the sunny afternoon is ominous with the gradual approach of the dreadful night.
The shadow of the chimney moving across the lawn is
the silent enemy drawing always nearer through the
doomed sunshine, and I dread the coming darkness. Night
will envelop the house like a hostile spell, closing in, sti-

fling, besieging us as an active presence till the morning.
It is absurd, but

> *the mind, mind has mountains; cliffs of fall*
> *Frightful, sheer, no-man-fathomed. Hold them*
>   *cheap*
> *May who ne'er hung there.*

The children would certainly hold them cheap if they
knew, for they do not mind the dark in the slightest.
They go upstairs at night unconcerned, to fetch a toy
from their bedroom, to run the water for their bath, not
feeling in the least that to go into a black room and turn
on the light is to brave some strange invisible enemy.
"No, thank you," they say, when I make some excuse for
leaving them a dim light till morning. "No, I like the light
out and my door shut." In fact they seem untroubled by
most of the usual fears and horrors. Not only the dark,
but they are indifferent to spiders, they like snakes, they
are not disgusted by lice, they delight in thunderstorms.
So that one wonders how many of our supposedly deep-
seated horrors are only picked up from our companions.

On long Summer evenings one can retreat into sleep
before the fear of the night begins, but in Winter, when
the daylight seems only an incident in the established
dark, there is no escape. There are nights when we feel
that the light will never come back, that some dark end
of the world has closed in on us, some ancient hostile
power. So that when it should be morning again we shall
"wake and feel the fell of dark, not day," and all die lost
and frightened in the endless night.

> *This is the way the world ends*
> *Not with a bang but a whimper.*

AUTUMN

But then, in the sudden morning (for one sleeps despite the fear) there is the blessedly reassuring everyday world, even the spade one left out after digging the day before, there, incredibly, the whole time.

As a child I used to think how dreadful it was for the trees that they must be out in the dark all night, that they were rooted, and could not run away when they were frightened. Every tree, I suppose, a ridiculous chained Andromeda. How brave the cows and sheep were, I thought, to stay out alone, and dogs seemed astonishing heroes because they faced so unconcernedly the unknown terrors of the dark. For we take it for granted that all dogs are brave, but they are not. The Farmer has a black retriever, charming and friendly, with manners as irreproachable as the Farmer's own, and a level of intelligence quite unsuitably high for a dog. She will do everything expected of her in the way of barking, rouse the sleeping house, set off the neighbouring dogs in all the farms for miles around, but she will no more go out to challenge a noise in the night than I would myself.

EARLY Autumn this year has been Keats's mellow season, "Close bosom-friend of the maturing sun." But it is Shelley now, his wild west wind and "the steep sky's commotion." And the children are out in the tossing orchard, bowling hoops over the tussocky grass.

The hoops arrived this morning, a present from an old friend who sends always the exactly right imaginative gift, and the children chase them delightedly, blown along in the westerly gale. Such generous open gestures of flying arms and hair, of thrown-out chests, and legs like wild pistons. And overhead the rooks soar and tumble, and the leaves come swirling down.

We have bowled them into the wind, and stopped to

get our breath for laughing. We have skipped in them, and thrown them to come back like boomerangs. I have spun them round my waist as I used to, doing a hula-hula dance to keep them up. But I can no longer run through a running hoop—I must have been much smaller and nimbler in my own hoop days.

They are beautiful, the springing, spinning planes, balanced and fragile, with a strange, intense stillness within the taut band. For these are not dead iron hoops tamely made to shape, but wood bent and fastened, alive and resilient with the need to straighten out again.

The little boys of the city where I lived as a child had iron hoops which clattered along the pavements. They never went astray as my wooden one did, they never bounced at the pavement edges, they never ran away downhill. How could they when they were held firmly by their owner in a hooked iron stick? I scorned these tethered hoops only a little less than I scorned their equally tethered owners. I would have run hoopless for ever rather than harness myself to such a tame and ugly contraption. Perhaps it was sour grapes, for I never learnt to manage an iron hoop, but I think not entirely. I felt the same about trams and the new buses which were then first appearing in our city. Buses were wooden hoops, I thought. They could wander all over the road, they went fast or slow as they liked, and they bounced about on their springs and rubber tires. But trams, the iron hoops, I hated, clanging along their predestined road-centre rails. I disliked their smell, a curious metallic smell which I have never met since, and the way they made my feet tickle through the boards and iron. But the new buses were expensive, sometimes as much as sixpence for a ride, and a tram would take you to the furthest edge of the town's industrial sprawl for only three halfpence.

AUTUMN

So it was mostly trams, but these are wooden hoops, the biggest and bounciest kind, as they should always be. Exciting with their invisible planes implied, and subtly juxtaposed as they pass each other. Paul Nash might have painted them, as he paints the planes of the ladder in his picture called *March*, but he would not have caught their tension. Degas, perhaps, but not Renoir, for all the little girl with the hoop in *Parapluies*.

F OR a week now the children have had whooping-cough, and are unexpectedly ill, for I had thought it was only another mild childish ailment like the rest. All night long they cough and choke and vomit, and wake crying with fear to feel the attacks coming on.

It is one of the subtler tortures to watch one's children ill. Hostages to fortune, Bacon calls them, and so they are. They are vulnerable and defenceless, and we can only watch. It is like having one's heart put out on a dish and one can do nothing at all to save it, only sit by and watch.

I would willingly cough all night to save them five minutes, but all I can do by sitting up from midnight to dawn is hold their hand when the attacks come on. Ill children should not be nursed by mothers, who wear themselves out in this useless misery of pity, but by some kindly stranger bringing only the sympathy and skill needed to help them.

Of course they will get well again. All families go through this and worse. But still a week of sleepless nights and fretful days does not encourage any sense of proportion. And even so, the sense of proportion is an intellectual support merely, the bony skeleton which holds us upright, but saves us not at all from the agonies of the flesh.

The real world now is bounded by the sick-room walls, and all beyond is only echoes, remote as a dream. Yet even so, so shut in and confined, so sick with anxiety, there is still a clear, small voice of rebellion saying that this is no fit occupation for human beings created for their intelligence, that illness is no more than a tiresome accident of our animal state, that we should not let our reasonable life be overwhelmed by these physical and emotional upheavals.

The coughing begins just before midnight, so I go to bed now with the children, and get up again at half past eleven for the night. They seem less frightened if they find me there when they wake, to help them sit up and find the basin, and there is nothing else I can do.

Poor Peter is unexpectedly dignified in his stubborn self-respect, for he almost never loses control of himself, even in the worst attacks. Only sometimes, roused violently to choke and vomit before he is properly awake, he cries quietly and helplessly, sighing: "O dear, O dear" in a tired, unchildlike voice.

This afternoon he had an attack much worse than usual for the day, for the daytime fits are generally mild. And hopelessly, from fields of sad experience, "O dear," he said. "O dear. It feels like the night."

The nights are endless and dreadful for all of us, and this is the worst time of all the year to be up in the dark. The rain weeps on the windows, and the house is cold and unhappy with the threat of the long Winter ahead. Worst of all is the time when the first light begins, a dead, slatey grey, no more than a lessening of the darkness, but real enough to make the lamplight tawdry and the tangled heads and crumpled bedclothes unbearably sad.

My eyes are tight and sore with tiredness like skin after sunburn, and I feel that in one night I have grown a hundred years old. I comfort myself with remembering the

serenity of Stowe Park in the sunshine, the gardens at
Versailles, and I pin up a plan of Paris on the bedroom
wall ("Look," says John of the Tour Eiffel. "Look,
there's the Meccano Tower"). For I need badly to be
reminded that though I must live in this squalor, man is
"noble in reason! how infinite in faculty! in form and
moving how express and admirable! . . . the beauty of
the world!" and not merely a suffering animal. I long, as
I long often, but never so despairingly as now, for Baudelaire's world of *là-bas.*

> *Là tout n'est qu'ordre et beauté,*
> *Luxe, calme et volupté.*

Always, wakened in the night by a child's cry, there is a
moment of intense, unreasoning terror, some unconscious
atavistic dread perhaps of enemies in the dark, so that for
an uncontrolled second I lie rigid with fear, before my
real world reassures me, and with a sigh of habit and already of boredom I stumble into dressing-gown and slip-
pers, stuff the bedside book into my pocket, and am at the
cotside before John has even time to cry out twice.

The bedside book is one of the very few compensations
of this night nursing, for I have never had the gift of cat-
napping, dropping off to sleep at will in odd half-hours. I
shall put it on my list of desirable improvements. And
since, once wakened, I am awake for good, I read Henry
James. This I scarcely dare do in normal times, for though
I can resist starting any of them, even that perfect miniature *The Awkward Age*, once I have begun I drown
completely. The beds go unmade, the meals uncooked,
the children might be lost all day without my noticing, so
real is his created world beside the irrelevant muddle
around me.

AUTUMN

The only way, I find, once embarked, is to read without stopping, sleep in the unmade beds (which I do not notice and the children do not mind), feed us all on milk and bread, and simply read through until I come out at the other end and his world fades, leaving only a faint echo of his involved style, so that I listen to myself placing the pernickety commas as I order bread from the baker.

But this is a better way. I forbid myself absolutely to open any Henry James except when I am up in the night. Measles and *The Ambassadors*, chicken-pox and *The Golden Bowl*, whooping-cough and *The Wings of the Dove*; but whooping-cough goes on too long, and *The Wings of the Dove* is really too sad, even by Chekhov's standards.

They both of them, Chekhov and Henry James, have the same deep consciousness of how pitifully we are all hurt by life. Of how there is no need of outside disaster (it is only in James's earlier and cruder stories that events happen from outside his characters), but that our own human weaknesses and indecisions are more than enough for tragedy.

For the moment, though, it is not Henry James but *Richard II*. I sit down to read it for the sixth time or so, and always it is a brand-new story and I wonder what is going to happen. I struggle to sort out the characters, turning back at every new entrance to my finger kept at Dramatis Personæ, and my head ringing with so many urgent voices all talking at once. Then someone says: "graved in the hollow ground" and I know that soon the king will say to his sad departing queen: "We make woe wanton with this fond delay," and that I have heard it all before, and forgotten. And that of the drama and characters, no more will remain for me this time than all the other times I have read it, but only scraps and snatches of poetry.

I realize humbly that I have no historical sense at all, and I know it must be a sad loss, losing so many echoes. Sometimes, with a conscious person, I catch them faintly, and realize how much I miss. One day walking along the Loire between two historical friends, I caught for a few seconds their feeling of the land belonging to its people, of the history lived so intimately over its hills and valleys. Only pre-Conquest history I remember a little, because it is vague and simple and half legend, and because it has the charm of being mostly out of doors.

It is my scale which is too big, for though I almost never remember that Englishmen have in their history the Plantagenet Kings, I am always conscious that man has in his background Devonian fishes and a forward-looking tree-mouse and men who painted bulls on cave walls.

Perhaps it is only men who have this feeling for history —though that is nonsense, of course. But certainly their father is glad that our children are boys to carry on his name, while I care not a scrap. I am only glad of boys because I should not know how to bring up girls, for girls alarm me. At adolescence they enter a world of intimate personalities where I have never been able to follow them. Whatever the sensibility that is needed to approach them, I seem not to have it. Once I minded bitterly, but it seems not to matter very much any more since I am to live in a household of men.

Tonight the trains sound very close, snorting and whistling, and it must be going to rain. It is odd how everyone who lives in England believes that to hear the trains is a sign of rain. No matter which way the railway lies, north, west, south, or east, if the trains sound nearer than usual as they rattle through the dark, if the puffing and clanging come close and clear on the wind, then it will rain. Quite certainly.

I have never noticed that it does rain, particularly—only that everyone believes it will. "There," they say, when the shower comes rattling on the windows, "I knew it would rain when we heard the trains." And as we all do, they forget their prophecies on all the other windy nights when the skies stay clear.

But tonight the trains sound so close that they must be at the bottom of the garden, and it will rain before morning. And sitting by the dark window waiting for it to begin, I think how strange it is that I am not frightened. Fear of the night, it seems, is a tenuous life of the imagination easily crowded out by real things, by anxiety and tiredness and the world of the sick-room. I go down unthinking into the dark well of the house for fresh hot-water bottles, caring nothing for the kitchen with its four black windows on to the night. I am indifferent to the creaking on the stairs, the tapping behind the walls, the rustling in the chimney—all the sounds of the house at night—for it is only quiet just before dawn, that low ebb when men die.

Someone, I think it was Edgar Allan Poe, said that we are only strong enough to conquer our emotions because our emotions are not strong enough to conquer us. Written down as equations of x and y, it seems an obvious truth, yet it is a cynical statement for aspiring human beings. It makes of the loves we govern only indifference, it belittles our virtues because we do not feel the pull of evil, it turns courage to insensibility.

And perhaps it is. Certainly these nights I am not brave, only busy in my other selves of anxious mother and patient nurse, too preoccupied for the intangible terrors of the dark to reach me. Like the children, I am wrapped up in my own affairs, and the shadowy fears can find no way into my consciousness. I am not brave at all, but unreceptive, and perhaps the real heroes too are simply not frightened. I can only hope so for their own comfort.

And perhaps the way with any obsession is to ignore it simply. Not to fight it, since it draws strength from any contact with us, whether hostile or friendly, but to busy one's mind with something else. Not to go round locking the doors but to turn on the wireless. Hate, after all, as lovers have always known, is not the opposite of love, but only the other side of the penny. It can link us almost as closely as love with the person we detest. It is indifference which is the different currency.

I SAID I would go in again and say good night to John before he went to sleep, but unpardonably I forgot. So twice in the night he woke up sobbing because I had not come, and in between, one imagines, he wandered lost in unhappy dreams. I can only be relieved that when the children are well they are cheerfully independent.

They have coughed for two weeks now, and we are all exhausted. I suppose everyone has his own way of making tiredness bearable, and mine is to keep my head above water and watch it happen. A little tired, and I am irritable, *agacée*. Everything annoys me: the telephone bell, the pots which need such constant washing up, the tractor starting up noisily in the yard. The company of the children in the same room is an irritation scarcely to be endured for five minutes. More tired, the irritation goes, and I become as sentimental as the most melting Victorian heroine, seeing my world through an emotional haze which has very little to do with sense. But really exhausted, I am simply unnaturally kind. I do whatever is needed with quite pathetic patience, overwhelmed with gratitude at the least kindness in return. Perhaps this is how I should be if I were drunk; but how can anyone believe the mind is independent of the body?

Still I am comforted a little through the interminable nights by a plaster head of a Cambodian Buddha which I brought back once from Paris, embarrassing the customs officers who went through my bags looking for silk stockings. The eyes are closed, but not in sleep, and it smiles and smiles through the darkness, a drugged and secret smile, as if it knew all this from long ago, and none of it matters. If we must make for ourselves anthropomorphic gods, this surely is how they should be, serene and wise and happy. When things seem really too dismal a confusion to deal with at the time, I sit with the Buddha on the edge of my grave and look back. And the things which matter are very clear among the things which do not, since all the important things are the same, and that is to be happy.

Happy. Such an ingenuous word, like children clapping their hands, but for all that more elusive and unpredictable than the rare kingfisher we always hope to see on the stream. Given paints and canvas, we cannot paint a picture, nor given the materials of happiness, achieve the state. Yet what other test can there be of a successful life? Being powerful, or useful, or rich, or good are only our individual ways of being happy, and of no value in themselves unless we are so. Good works for others only shift on to the others the responsibility of being happy. Reforms and discoveries come of themselves when the time is ready for them, from many sources at once. Anything useful we do could be done equally well by a dozen other people.

And who shall decide which are the reforms and what

is useful? Medicine perhaps? But doctors have kept alive
a generation of pathetic old people in a western society
which has no place for them. Preventive medicine is so
multiplying the population of the world that soon there
will not be food enough to keep us all alive. And in a few
thousand years, since it obstructs the evolutionary law
of the survival of the fittest, medicine may have produced
a race of monsters.

Yet doctors may well be content, feeling their work
useful, for we can judge nothing but our own personal
happiness, and only that is valid. Which makes it only
more difficult, and not more simple, and is why I have to
sit so often these years on the edge of my grave.

Some people are born with the gift of being happy for
the moment, but most of us need some sort of plan to
give our lives coherence. And since human beings are
mostly virtuous, we need to feel good and useful, that
others are happy round us, that no one suffers through
our doing. All this besides being warm and fed, and
healthy, and occupied, and a dozen other luxuries. Small
wonder that happiness is a fitful state.

Looking back, it is the things we have not done which
we regret, the chances lost from diffidence or cowardice
or meanness of spirit. The foolish things we did and so
regretted at the time look, from this graveyard distance,
only generous and pathetic. And I would not in any case
go back to live any of it over again, even if I could. Such
a weary effort when one had got this far along, like going
back to the beginning of a party when one had just
reached the end. Besides, it is precisely from the best
parties that one goes away satisfied. I still look forward to
what is left, but to have even the happiest years over
again would be as if in the middle of a meal one were sud-

denly offered a second helping of a course already over. Delicious it was certainly, but one had finished it and gone on to the next.

"But," someone argues, "there are more important things than being happy. We can work For the Good of Others," that evasive phrase. So we can, but we should still recognize that fundamentally we do it because we want to do it, because it is our own virtuous way of being happy. And the happiness of the others is almost completely unpredictable.

We had a calendar once when I was a child, with a quotation for every day. "Thoughts for the Day" it was called, and delightfully incongruous they must have been, for they always are, and very moral. One I still remember: "There is nothing either good or bad, but thinking makes it so."

It surely might be quoted to the over-optimistic social planners who perhaps do not read *Hamlet*, and who hope to make the whole world happy. For even supposing we can measure happiness in calories and council houses, man is still an endlessly adaptable animal; we grow quickly used to the conditions we live in, good or bad. If they are good, we become more susceptible to minor woes, if bad, more callous to real hardships. We of this squeamish age are as offended by an outside privy as the eighteenth century by streets which were open sewers, yet we accept horrors of modern war which would have appalled them. And here, while half the world is homeless and wretched, here I live snugly with my children. We are safe, we are not frightened, we have enough to eat and wear, we can make our lives as we like in a beautiful house and country, yet it seems to me a hardship that I should sit up at night for three weeks to nurse them through a childish ailment.

Altering the stimulus will blunt or refine the instrument, but not for long alter the strength of the reaction. Only for a short time in new conditions, while we are learning the suitable intensity of response, there is a period of heightened awareness, pleasure or pain. And it is the response which is our emotion and which in the end changes least. We simply alter the gears of the machine to suit the journey. Prisoners have been happy, they tell us, yet Keats was wretched only to remember that women died of cancer.

If we take a starving man from a hovel and put him in a cottage with enough bread to eat, there will be an interval of blissful content before he sighs for a house with bay-windows and unrationed butter. But it is useless to think that that would satisfy him either, for once achieved he would want a pillared portico and champagne suppers.

What the outside observer considers he ought to feel in the way of happiness is really quite irrelevant. What a pity it will be if what the social planners consider the planned-for should feel turns out to be equally irrelevant. For if man were not fundamentally a discontented animal, there seems no reason why he should not still be swinging through the trees and eating monkey-nuts.

I know that if I had enough coal to bank up our miserly fire, I should still want to sun-bathe in the garden in the middle of Winter, and when we had no coal at all, I was no more discontented.

Indeed there was one bad Winter when for three freezing weeks we had no fuel of any kind. Certainly we were miserable at first, so cold that we were conscious all the time of outer space beyond the thin shell of tiled roof which separated us. Human beings, one came to feel, should live in cities and huddle together against the cold and dark of eternity. But we soon accepted the cold house, soon got used to wearing coats and gloves and scarves indoors, and the children so used to being muffled up with layer upon layer of wool that they tumbled about on purpose for the fun of not feeling the bumps through the padding.

It had the advantage, too, that we lived as much out of doors as we do in Summer, for, like the Summer, it was no colder in the garden than in the house, and the frosty country was a delicate delight. Cooking certainly was more difficult, for since we had only a Primus stove and very little kerosene, our meals varied rather narrowly between hot soup with bread and cheese, and hot milk with bread and jam. No one, understandably, came to have tea with us, but if they had, we should have had to chip the frozen milk from the jug and ladle it into their tea-cups in lumps to melt.

But the cooking, too, came to matter very little. The real hardship was the water. We had nothing but one cold tap in the kitchen sink, kept thawed by burning candles under it day and night. But it needed more will-power than we could manage to wash properly in water which was spikey with ice as soon as it ran into the bowl. I longed and longed for a bath, not only to be clean, but to feel myself uncluttered by so many layers of clothes.

That, looking back, is the only trouble I remember vividly. I wanted a bath. It is too frivolous even to mention without shame to people who listen for the knock on the door at three in the morning. That and the gold-fish. For one particularly Arctic night there was a crack like a gun, and next morning the children found their poor loved fish frozen into a solid globe of ice on the windowsill, with the shattered glass bowl all over the kitchen floor. There were dreadful scenes of weeping, but we thawed the fish out over the candle, and they went on as before with their seemingly aimless life—and have done ever since.

As for us, we were all three absurdly healthy, the sun shone and shone from a blue sky, dazzling on the frost which never melted, and we were curiously content. I think it must be the same in any extreme, hot as well as cold. Life is serenely simple. We must keep warm. Nothing else. All the vague anxieties and dissatisfactions disappear. The whole end of living is to keep warm in the cold, and as that was easy enough in the dry, windless air, we were confident and happy, with every day a pleasant feeling of achievement.

There was very little to do without water. No washing, no cooking, no cleaning. The household was on holiday. We lived out of doors, and fed the tame, starving birds, and since we could not keep still unless we went to bed, having no way to get warm again if we once got cold, we went for long walks in the enchanted country with flocks of red-wings keeping us hungry and hopeful company along the frosted hedges.

Tonight too has seemed friendly and comfortable after the last weeks. Almost a pleasant night it has been, and only because there was a lantern backwards and forwards in the yard where the Farmer was delivering a cow in calf. I could hear her moaning quietly. The new bull must go, he says, the calves are born with heads too big.

The children have coughed as usual, the house is hostile with cold, there is nothing ahead but more nights of coughing, and beyond that the Winter, and beyond that the war. Yet because there has been a dim light at the bottom of the garden the night has seemed happy, so receptive can one become to the slightest comfort.

A U T U M N

In the morning, I thought, the Farmer will call across as he goes through the orchard to let out his hens: "How are the boys?" for he never calls them the children, but always the boys, seeing in them, perhaps, the sons he has never had. "How are they?" I thought he would say. "I saw their light on in the night." And it was pleasant to think of the morning, with another night over and behind us. "And how is the cow?" I thought I should call back through the kitchen window. "I saw your lantern in the yard."

But I care not at all for the poor cow. I am glad of the calf's big head, and glad to think of all the other cows in the herd, heavy and swaying and near their time, knowing I shall have the lantern's company for nights to come. Though perhaps my nursing will soon be over, for the children sleep more at night now, looking curiously younger as sleeping children always do.

Young people look younger asleep, they bathe at night, and they like to eat great quantities of green apples. Old people look older asleep, they bathe in the morning, and they do not like green apples at all.

That was how I used to tell the sheep from the goats, but there are other ways of recognizing the young in heart. The enthusiasms of the old are not positive as youth's are, but negative. When they are roused, it is always against some iniquity, some extravagance, some change which came too late for them to accept. It may be the Income Tax or Modern Women or Picasso. It may even be motor-cars, for I have a treasured friend who still thinks of bowling down to Brighton in a carriage at a spanking trot. But he is not old at all, only old-fashioned, which is different and delightful.

The young, too, are violent attackers, since it is no business of enthusiastic youth to see too many sides to any question. But they attack the old restrictions with their new ideas, and if they are often as opinionated as the old, it is a different sort of closed mind. One is a house we cannot get into because it is locked, the other because so strong a wind of enthusiasm rushes through the open doors.

When I find myself decrying new fashions, and the working-man, and modern art, I shall know, not that the world is going from bad to worse, but that I am growing old. For the world has always gone from bad to worse for anyone over the critical dividing age when Utopia ceases to be in some cloudy future and becomes the Good Old Days.

Yet the old can be tolerant when they are wise, and with a positive, adult tolerance which the young know nothing of. The young have no business to be tolerant, for them it is only a relaxing of standards, a good-natured letting slip of the rules, and not an imaginative acceptance of differences. For the young judge everyone by themselves, not each person by his own separate standards, as one must. Even with people they love, they only slowly and painfully learn to accept the differences.

We are changed by loving another person, we see the world through their eyes, not our own, accept for a time their different standards; and though in the end we go back to our own conception, it is never again quite so clear-cut, nor we quite so ruthless.

And old people are pathetic, not because they are weak or ugly, but because in the west they have no place, and are not respected. The New World is for the young, who are seldom kind.

Being between the generations, I am still young enough to be flattered if older people seek me out, feeling that with them is urbanity and experience, and that the young

are only awkwardly callow, being too near my own
youth for the charm of difference. But I know that in
time I too shall be humble and touched if young people
enjoy my company, and it is disheartening.

So many of the finest old people have sad faces. Not
because their lives have been sad, but because an unconscious settled melancholy has worn through to the surface of their cheerful faces, like the shape of underlying
rocks. It is as if they had watched existence for a long
time and found it incurably unhappy. For we all live in
a small, fragile world of our own making, live cheerfully
for the most part, but still it is better not to look out too
often to see where we are going, since we are helplessly
afloat on a swift river which carries us to death. Even
the children have made years of the downstream journey,
and passed already landscapes they can never see again.
Some in the end drown gracefully, some make a fuss,
but we are all alike engulfed and forgotten.

And it is not comfortable to realize that our pathetic
human pleasures are only flowers on the banks of the
inexorable river, that the plans and ideals we live by are
mirages which keep us travelling hopefully to the an-
nihilating grave. We do best to keep the doors and windows firmly shut around our little world, and not let
Shakespeare or world wars or the rest batter them down
too often.

From the highest windows of this house we can see,
on clear nights, the brightness of the air-raids on London,
forty miles away beyond the hills—flares and search-
lights, bomb and gun flashes, and once the sullen red
glow of fire. I have watched it for hours, crouching on
Peter's bed as he slept unconscious that his future was
being decided out there in the coloured flashes like distant fireworks. I would wrap myself in his eiderdown and

watch, only from a ridiculous feeling that it somehow helped, or perhaps paid for our privilege of safety out here, if I did not sit indifferent by the fire with my book.

It weighs upon the heart that he must think
What uproar and what strife may now be stirring
This way or that way o'er these silent hills.

So I stayed at the window like Coleridge, like the passenger in a motor-car who watches the road as carefully as the driver himself, even though he has no possible control of the driving.

There was one culminating night when for hour after hour the flashes were vivider than anything before. I knew no city and no people could survive such destruction, I felt the London I loved was disappearing, and the life I had planned for us all was tumbling in ruins while I watched.

The morning wireless brought good news for bad. The bigger flashes had been our bigger guns, and not the enemy's bigger bombs, and London was discreetly jubilant. But nothing altered the night. I had lost an unconscious belief that the life I knew would go on again when it was all over: a lost innocence I could never recover, for the emotions of a great war change and develop like a growing plant. At least they do for the watchers, and I am only humble, having never been in danger.

First there is fear, not so much that one will be hurt personally, but that evil forces are loose in the world, breeding hatred and cruelty. Then for a time there is anger: if we are hit, we will hit back—a confident patriotism with simple rights and wrongs.

This does not last long in wars where it is hard to tell one side from the other in the universal misery. For pity is the overwhelming emotion of wars, pity that human creatures, groping pathetically for happiness, should be driven blindly to such suffering.

Yet even pity dies in the end, in an immense weariness that such things should happen. If I were a god and these were my creatures, I would sweep us all away and leave the world green again.

We do better to stay indoors, for infinity waits outside all our windows, and not only Baudelaire's, though it was he who said it. "*Je ne vois qu'infini par toutes les fenêtres.*" And ordinary people are not made to look out on infinity too often. We may walk confidently, blind-fold on a tight rope over empty space, but if we once realize it is not the safe pavement under our feet, we are lost. Drowned in melancholy. If we could somehow ex-press it, write Hamlet's soliloquies, or Hopkins's sonnets, or Dido's farewell song to Æneas, then it might be bear-able. If we could transmute our cosmic sadness into for-mal art, we could keep it at a distance, confront it, and come to terms, not suffer within ourselves this burden of melancholy pity too overwhelming for the frail hu-man mind. So I look out of the window no oftener than I must, and arrange flowers on the windowsill instead.

It is three weeks now since the children started to cough, and at last they are getting better. Already Peter's face is losing the shadow of illness which I so dread and so love in him, and John begins to laugh again for nothing at all but his own high spirits. This morning at dawn he heard the sparrows twittering. "Dardy. Listen"—a voice of astonished delight. "Listen. I can hear a nightingale."

Two or three nights of sleeping for us all, and whoop-ing-cough will be only another of the difficulties behind us and forgotten. And I shall give us all a present as a reward: I will have a new window put in the house.

A U T U M N

There are three new ones already since we came, two small ones for the children, and a low one down to floor-level in my bedroom, so that I can lie in bed and look at the barley-field as well as the stream on the other side of the house.

The next one is to be in the kitchen. There are enough, of course, with four already, but still there is a special view of the orchard which it seems a pity not to bring into the house. I shall find an old window in a sale, and call on the old man who lives beyond the station. He will do any odd jobs (even the oddest without comment) so long as no one hurries him. Then one day when he feels like it, he will come along with his hammer and chisel. A good hard tap anywhere cn the walls, and the bricks fall out into the garden. It is a very convenient house for anyone who likes putting in windows. And by evening —for although my old man never hurries, he works fast —we shall have our new kitchen view, and the early sun next morning.

I suppose they make the house cold, my windows, but with so little warmth to keep in in any case, it scarcely seems to matter. Besides, I tell myself that the luxury of the Elizabethans was a luxury of the mind, and so must mine be. Velvet and cloth-of-gold, larks' tongues and peacocks. Of comfort they knew nothing at all, and we all of us now live in greater physical luxury than Renaissance princes, who never heard of baths with running water, or good roads to travel on, or fresh food all Winter. And I can never walk through the marble glories of Versailles without thinking how cold it all must have been, and how smelly.

So we will have our new window, though the children are not better yet, only recovering. But they no longer drop off to sleep exhausted after each fit of coughing.

This morning I composed John with a smooth bed and shut eyes, and told him drowsy stories hopefully. But when I stopped, thinking him asleep, a polite and wakeful voice asked: "Have you finished?"

"Yes," I said, cross.

His eyes flew open as if they were on springs and he had only held them closed to please me. He waved his hands under my nose. "Look. My hands are going so fast you can't see them." But who can be interested in optical illusions at five in the morning? I left him to find his own way to sleep.

I HAVE been conscious all day of how strange it will be to go back into the world with a husband and two sons, and how I have had no chance at all to get used to it on this moated island with my husband away. For all attitudes and relationships will be changed now that other people see me, not as myself, but as someone's wife and someone's mother.

Before one is married, all the world, and young men in particular, seem not to be able to think of young women without thinking also of weddings, as if one's only status and occupation were in being an unmarried girl. So that the only relationship I had learnt how to manage was being more or less in love. But now that is no use any longer, and I must learn to talk to my new acquaintances about schools for our respective children.

Well, at least they will listen, which my young men infuriatingly never did in the old days when I talked to them about Shelley's metaphysics. But small wonder, and how sensible of them to think of something else.

John is well again, and Peter well enough for us both to sleep most of the night if I put his bed beside mine and hold his hand. This he insists on, for he believes it is a certain charm to ward off coughing, and wakes up anxiously however cautiously I try to slide my hand away.

But it really is too cold. I wonder if I could wear a glove, though it scarcely seems fitting. For I cannot help feeling one should not wear gloves at a sick-bed; it destroys the proper atmosphere. However, anything at all is better than having children in the same bed with me. They toss and wriggle and seem all painful knees and elbows. A horse in bed could scarcely be more uncomfortable.

How I long for the luxury of having my nights to myself again. To close the door firmly on household and children, and settle down with a hot-water bottle. Even two hot-water bottles, as the ultimate height of luxury, and a book to read until I fall asleep till morning. I cannot believe that I was ever dissatisfied with evenings so uneventful.

But now at last I know just what passed between Cinderella and the Prince, what happened in the fairy-tales when they married and lived happily ever after. For I have finished reading Henry James, and what are his greatest novels but quite wonderfully elaborated fairy-tales? Adult, ironic, with a texture infinitely subtle, but still, as making for the highest art, fairy-tales.

Here are the princes, the innocent girls, the mysterious beautiful ladies, the secret villains, the riches, the gardens, the palaces, the foreign lands of authentic fairy-tale. For we never in ordinary life meet creatures so wonderful. So lovely, so charming, so wise. Even his heroes and villains are subtle and various. Not that Henry James deals in villains in his late great novels. Like real life, he manages his tragedies quite devastatingly well without.

It is not simple any more as it used to be once upon a

time when they all lived happy ever after. There are ironies, twists of good and bad, the hero playing the villain, and the villain the hero, complications we never dreamed of in the black and white world of childhood morality.

But still for our delight there are the same wondrous creatures, the same accepted plots. There is Mr. Strether, dearest Mr. Strether, who went to rescue a young man from Fairyland, only to fall in love himself with the Fairy Queen (for what else is Mme de Vionnet?), so that he in turn, an ironic addition, must be rescued from the enchantment by protectors sturdily impervious to the spell. And how quite horribly impervious Henry James makes them, his successful American family.

Mr. Strether's motives for going back in the end are no clearer now than they were of old in the fairy-tale, nothing but a vague moral compulsion. And we are left with the same wonder as to how he settled back to disenchanted small-town life after his dream of Fairyland. Poor Mr. Strether, for, like everyone else who meets him, we grow very fond of him.

It is not only Mr. Strether's future, for there is always the wonder of what happens to Henry James's people when he leaves them. It is one of his greatnesses that they go on living and changing after his story ends. And he leaves us with such dreadful vistas, such horrible implied probabilities: of Mme de Vionnet deserted, of Kate Croy grown hard and rich and bitter, of poor Nanda with her broken heart (which we believe in because she is quiet), of Caroline, who for all her wickedness holds our sympathy against Aggie Verver's over-saintly virtue, of Caroline tied to a husband whose subtleties of torture one cannot even forgive as being unconscious. They none of them, indeed, live happy ever after, but then these are tales for *les grandes personnes*, not for children.

Since Henry James's characters live in their own right, and not as puppets to express his ideas (as Bernard Shaw's do, for instance), it is possible to look at them through the eyes of other writers, to realize them with a different vision. We can see what Mauriac might have made of *The Wings of the Dove*. By an effort of simplifying (and oddly too by vulgarizing) we can imagine *The Awkward Age* written by Jane Austen. But as always, imagining Jane Austen with any plots but her own, what we see most clearly is how much is outside her range, a limitation we are never conscious of while reading her, so perfect is she as an artist.

So that it is not Henry James's characters which express what he wants to say, not his plots, not certainly his "message" (for he is a novelist and not a preacher), but his vision of his people, the way he looks at their lives. The characters, the background, the plots—these are only incidental. They are what he happens to know. As Cézanne happened to know the Mont Sainte Victoire, and painted it over and over. Yet the mountain is an accident, and a hundred other views would have done as well. So would other settings have done for Henry James.

Yet still he is lucky in what he found: a cultured society in the peaceful age before the flood, with leisure and composure for sensitive living. The noise from the world outside does not drown the quiet personal voices as it does for us, and his people are living at the right intensity for human beings, as we are not. Pianos are meant to be played by fingers, not by sledge-hammers. Violence makes them less and not more eloquent. And we humans are made to respond to intimate stimuli, to personal emotions and domestic situations, not to world wars and mass wretchedness. Beaten with sledge-hammers, we have no more to say than the jangled piano. Only by concentrating on the single muted detail does our response become significant, the picture of the child left crying after the bombing, the story of the idealist who sees his ideals betrayed in *Les Silences de la Mer*.

It is a lesson the adventure writers never learn, and why they are therefore seldom interesting to adults. (For Conrad is enthralling because of his descriptive power, and not for what he describes.) Nor did Henry James learn the lesson straight away. The early novels are melodramatic, and proportionately less moving. *The Portrait of a Lady* almost qualifies for being the earliest of the great stories, but still the plot is too highly coloured, too unfelt. If all the stimuli were reduced to half, the reactions, oddly, would be doubly as convincing. It is the enlarging of people's sensibility which makes them interesting, not the enlarging of the accidents which happen to them.

Not long ago, on first finding Henry James and realizing how much I was having to read into him that was not set down on the page, I wondered in naïve conceit whether I were not perhaps supplying too much. But then I found the preface to *A Sense of the Past* and realized humbly that I catch no more than half the implications he throws out. I wonder if the most intelligent reader hears all the echoes he intended. For there are not only the echoes inside each story, how every word and look and gesture, every slightest situation, even the placing of guests in a room, so immediately reacts on everyone else. All the complications, in fact, for which one reads him—or (understandably) does not, for he can be tiresome on sunny mornings, like being tied up in spiders' webs.

But there are also the echoes between the four great novels—*The Awkward Age, The Ambassadors, The Golden Bowl, The Wings of the Dove*. Perhaps too *The Portrait of a Lady*, since the theme is the same. For they are all variations on a theme, not only of character, but of relationships and situations. It is as if they were a single work, each part enriching the others by a new interpretation.

There is the innocent girl—Nanda, the American daughter, Aggie, the Dove. There is an innocent man —Mr. Strether, Mr. Verver, Merton Densher, and Nanda's elderly friend. There is a charming amoral woman —Nanda's mother, Mme de Vionnet, Caroline, Kate Croy. There is a weak and charming man—Mr. Vanderbank, Chad, the Prince, Merton Densher.

Between them they act out the parts of hero and heroine, villain and villainess. But not as one expects. For our sympathies make Mme de Vionnet the heroine of *The Ambassadors*, and the innocent wronged American daughter the unconscious potential villainess. It is Mr. Verver, not the Prince, whom we feel to be the villain of *The Golden Bowl*, though his fellows in the other novels are the heroes.

Then there are ironic twists between the stories: Chad refuses an American fiancée who knows too little; Mr. Vanderbank will not have Nanda because she knows too much. With no scruples for himself he cannot face her worldliness, yet her saintly old friend finds her touchingly defenceless.

Merton Densher, dreamer and irresolute, is both hero and villain in *The Wings of the Dove*. And so it goes on and on. But surely some patient American could put them all in a file for us, with cross references. And he must include too that odd figure Henry James is so fond of—a kind of Greek chorus, an omniscient woman of superhuman perception and understanding, who hears all the echoes the rest of us miss. She is Maria in *The Ambassadors*, Nanda's mother, the Dove's companion, and in *The Golden Bowl* a shadowy woman whose name (like most of the others) I have forgotten now that all the books have gone back to the library. They are never happier than when explaining what is going on, to the rest of the characters and incidentally to us as well. And I certainly, understanding, I suspect, no more than half what I should, am delighted to accept any help they like to offer.

AFTER breakfast the children went out to play in the sand-pit, for they are well again now at last, and their usual independent selves. But when the milk-lorry drove up to collect the churns half an hour later, Peter climbed down from between the drivers.

They had found him, they said, half a mile away down in the village, walking carefully along the edge of the road and carrying his red engine. Where was he going? they asked. He was taking his engine to the station to see the trains. Would he like to come back to the farm? No, thank you, he was going to the station. Would he like to come back to the farm sitting between the two drivers in the front of the lorry? This was obviously too much to resist, and I suppose he thought the station would still be there another day, so back he came.

This afternoon we all of us went to the station, as we do every Friday in the Winter, the children standing up at each end of their old pram, for it is too cold to wait while they walk, kicking stones which they lose in the hedge and insist on finding again. So I push them instead, and they ride standing, looking out on their world like princes, waving to the brick-lorries which thunder past along the main road.

At the station they watch for the lovely trains, and talk to the porters, who seem to them enviable and romantic figures, living so intimately with the railway. They climb on to the station bridge and pick out landmarks in the country round, they shout to each other from opposite platforms as if they were hailing each other from passing ships: "Hello, I can see you." "Yes, I can see *you*." Life at sea, after all, provides very little to talk about.

And I sit by the waiting-room fire and read the *New Statesman*, which is why we go on Fridays and not on any other day.

Every week the children promise each other that this time they will be brave enough to stand on the bridge while the express rushes past underneath, engulfing them in white mist. And every week, as soon as they see the white streak of smoke two miles away along the line, they scurry down the steps and flatten themselves against the waiting-room wall, their arms and legs spread out like starfish, and wait in delighted terror for the monster to come roaring past.

Luckily the express comes at tea-time, so there is no argument about when we shall go home, the afternoon having reached its regular and satisfying climax. Back we go for tea and bath and bed, and I am left with a long evening to settle down by the fire. Such luxury it seems, after the night watches, to read *Clarissa Harlowe* by the fire. And it does well for the early Winter, an indoor book, and, for all its intensity, of so leisurely a pace that it needs an unimpatient sense of long evenings ahead if we are not to skip too disastrously.

In French literature there is a tradition of novel-writing which I think we do not have in English. *Les Liaisons*

Dangereuses, Mademoiselle de Maupin, Adolphe, for example. It is a minute analysis of sexual relationships between people who have the leisure to give their whole time to it. The analysis is cynical, profound, and makes no obvious moral judgements, however much the plot may be turned for a conventional punishment of the villain.

The nearest we have in English, I think, is Richardson's *Clarissa Harlowe,* a muted and much less amusing *Liaisons Dangereuses.* And, as always, we like the villain best, for the heroines are such dreadful prigs. Good, of course, and meant to be all that is charming, but it is almost impossible to be so very virtuous and still be sympathetic. Some of the saints manage it, especially in Ireland, but then they are the rare elect. Not indeed elect in virtue, which is common enough, but in making virtue charming. Ordinary people seem to lose the gift with their childhood.

Tonight, interrupting the endless letters with his cry from a different outdoor world, the dog-fox is barking round the farm, calling to his vixen, which the Farmer shot this morning. A pity to do it, but really she presumed too much, strolling through the garden and looking in at the window to see that the Farmer was safely at tea before she massacred the hens.

She lived in a drain under the summer-house in the Farmer's garden; conveniently next door to the hens, and with a delightfully ironic fox for weather-vane on the roof to make her feel at home. It was no use to wait for the hunt to come and deal with her, for already she only stood still and watched us when we threw sticks to drive her off, stepping coolly aside to avoid them if we threw too close. Another week of good farmhouse food and she would have come trotting up to be patted.

AUTUMN

So they shot her, and now John says: "Bang, bang," whenever a fox is mentioned. And tonight the dog-fox calls her with three quick yaps like a puppy's, mournful at this distance, and she lies stretched out and stiff now on the floor of the great barn. We have all in turn picked her up by the tail, and all in turn exclaimed how heavy for so small an animal. For foxes are always smaller than one expects, as giraffes are always quite absurdly larger, their mild, unexpected heads towering astonishingly above their surroundings like ships in Southampton.

And at tea-time today, because of the fox and because they were still excited from the station, the children sang their game of Den-O even louder than usual.

I half remember it from when I was not much older than they are, a song someone used to sing me about a fox who:

Went out one wintry night,
And begged of the moon to give him light,
For he had many miles to go that night,
Before he came to his den-O, his den-O, his den-O,
* his den-O,*
For he had many miles to go that night,
Before he came to his Den-O.

Then there was a verse I have forgotten, but he must have come to a farmyard and stolen a goose, for:

Old Mrs. Slipper-Slopper jumped out of bed,
And out of the window she popped her head:
"John, John, John, the grey goose is gone,
And the fox is off to his den-O," etc.

I have no idea what happens after that, but even half-finished the children love it above all other songs. Mostly

I suppose because they know all about foxes and their habits, but also because it is the only tune they can sing, not being musical in the very least. Besides, they think Mrs. Slipper-Slopper is an exquisitely funny name, an excellent joke all by itself. So, feeling it to be their own special song, they have made a game of yelling the den-O's at the top of their voices.

"The fox is off," I start on the last line, they take a huge breath, and watch me with faces brilliant with excitement. Then: "Den-O, den-O, den-O!" we all shout, louder and louder, faster and faster, until they give in, helpless with laughter. We always sing it at the end of tea, for in the evening children grow as curiously excited as cats do at dusk, like a candle flaring high before it goes out, and suddenly they are both asleep.

And I am left with the evening for reading Richardson and Baudelaire. For really one must read Baudelaire here, in self-defence against a life of such unmitigated wholesomeness. Read him because he describes, not physical passion simply, though that is a rare enough gift, not affection certainly, but because he makes us share, more vividly than any other writer, the emotional obsessions of passion. And today, in sudden revolt against the nursery atmosphere I live in, I bought myself an orchid from the town, secretly guilty that so exotic a creature should be expected to travel in my bicycle basket.

It is not one of the sugar-fondant ones, not Cattleya pink (for really since Swann one can scarcely mention Cattleya), but it is not mauve, my orchid poised in the glass on the mantelpiece, not a witch disguised as a beautiful girl, but tawny and livid green, a witch self-confessed and much more beautiful. And it is strange, since wickedness is a moral quality, that a flower can give such a vivid feeling of evil. It is harmless, it does not sting, it is not even poisonous that I know of, yet it is a creature of such sinister malevolence that I am conscious all the time of its presence in the room, like a watchful animal waiting its chance to spring.

Magnolias too are evil flowers, but coarser and more primitive. Those luscious fleshy petals (they must surely be sweetish to eat, and with a texture like chicory salad) should have perished with some earlier larger-scale vegetation than our modern flowers so delicately contrived for tiny insects. Magnolias should be pollinated by huge gaudy butterflies, or dragonflies as large as birds, and it does not seem in the least surprising that there are fossil magnolias in cretaceous rocks with the dinosaurs and pterodactyls.

Orchids live too long, week after week, only growing imperceptibly paler each day, like the Autumn sun, until they are no more than ghosts of their evil selves. So that one day I must simply decide ruthlessly that my flower is dead, and turn it out. For creatures as glamorous as this should not stay so long, should last for a day only like a passion-flower, not stay until they become only ordinary and domestic. Neither is there anywhere here suitable for orchids to live. For this dear house has only one shortcoming that matters: there is no place at all for orgies. No room anywhere in the house where one can even imagine any kind of exotic behaviour.

Orgy is an adaptable word, like Shakespeare's Cleopatra, all things to all people, according to their secret and unsatisfied longings. And every house should have one room whose door will shut out the virtuous daylight world and enclose an island of delicious wickedness. Here there is nowhere. Nowhere for Baudelaire to bring his *"molle enchanteresse,"* nowhere one could hold Black Mass, or keep cats, or invite Huysmans to dine, or take opium, or keep snakes, or whatever one might fancy as a fascinating and secret sin.

And nowhere, I find, to put my Khmer head with the drugged and inward smile. For even my sitting-room, though oddly mysterious with its low ceiling and deep cupboard built into the wall, will not be dressed up in velvet and tiger-skins and shaded lights. The house presides always with so wise a tolerance that the excess turns to theatrical posturing.

But still it is a pity. I tried one endless gloomy Winter, stoked up the fire to languorous greenhouse heat, and filled my room with evil-smelling exotic flowers against the snow outside the windows. But it only looked cheerful, like a Christmas card, and now I know that it is no use trying. So I live resignedly, with only now and then an orchid in revolt, but still, in this austerity, overwhelmed by sudden nostalgias for lost unlikely pleasures.

Today it was table napkins. Thick, silky, creamy-coloured (they were damask, I suppose), and as big as tablecloths. When they come back again, they will be paperwhite and textureless, and in size the ungenerous minimum. And how I hate this niggardliness which has become almost second-nature for us all, so that I long for sweeping skirts yards and yards round the hem and bother the clothing coupons, for fires piled high with a month's coal-ration, and never, never again to scrape the paper the butter was wrapped in.

All I can do is save up the whole month's chocolate for us to eat all at once, and think of Marvell's garden:

> *What wond'rous Life is this I lead!*
> *Ripe Apples drop about my head;*
> *The Luscious Clusters of the Vine*
> *Upon my Mouth do crush their Wine;*

A U T U M N

The Nectaren and curious Peach [but *why* curious?]
Into my hands themselves do reach;
Stumbling on Melons as I pass,
Insnar'd with Flow'rs, I fall on Grass.

Even as a child, that had the special delight of lavish-
ness. Just as Christmas had, with so many presents that
no single surprise had to bear the strain of being all that
one had hoped for. If the first opened was not quite what
one had wanted, at Christmas it did not matter, as it *did*
matter, quite piercingly, on the other single-present occasions. But at Christmas there were endless other gifts
to fill up the gap, so that instead of being disappointed
at what each failed to be, one was pleased with what it
was and, bearing no intolerable burden of expectation,
it was a success.

Even the pile of presents was not all. After that there
was a bottomless stocking of smaller treasures, and then,
if there were still something quite special one had wanted
and not been given, there was Christmas money from distant uncles, and all the shops to choose from. I think we
had very few presents in between Christmases, but that
is how I would have all my pleasures—holidays, or snow,
or Summer weather, or flowers—stored up into lavish-
ness, so that the delight is untempered by the consciousness of there not being enough.

Well, we could have table napkins I suppose, but not
sensibly. For luxury is not to be bought with every coin.
Privation will do—we can go hungry to buy a lily—
but personal drudgery will not. At least, not one's own,
for I suppose all luxury is bought by someone's drudgery.
It is the old difficulty of combining Martha and Mary.
For here, too remote for laundry-vans to call, I must
wash and iron the table napkins myself, tired when the

children are at last in bed, turning what should be a casual
pleasure into a strenuous duty.

LAST night I was snatched violently awake by a tawny
owl which perched on the open window at my head and
hooted. I daresay it lived here before we did, like all the
rest, but still I hope it will not do it often. For it took
hours to calm myself to sleep again, and even today I
jump if a door so much as bangs.

If you cup your hands together and blow between
your thumbs, it makes a noise quite surprisingly like an
owl's hoot. Certainly the owls think so. I do it sometimes
from the garden these Autumn evenings when they are
at their noisiest, and they answer from all the fields
around, three and four together. Sometimes they come
to see what is happening, swooping into the elm trees by
the stream, or to the corner of the barn roof, darker
shapes in the darkness, like mediæval witches. But I have
never managed to deceive so near an audience. They
realize they have been tricked when I hoot at such close
range, and glide away again.

The orchard and the cow-yard at the end of the garden
must abound in mice, for the owls' fierce little hunting-
cry goes on all night round the house, and I long ago
learned to sleep through it. This is the "to-whit," I suppose, of the traditional "to-whit, to-whoo," but I have
never heard them join both sounds together, as they do
in all the best poems.

They have too—for I think it is all the tawny owls—a
raucous conversational caw, like a jackdaw's but hoarser,
and this slides sometimes deliciously into the liquid to-
whoo—oo—oo, like quicksilver from rough mercury ox-
ide (or whatever it was that one silvered mirrors with
in school chemistry lessons). Then there is a fast chatter

like a fiercer blackbird's alarm cry, a trill like a cuckoo's water-bubbling song, and a varied range of squawks and grunts and noises as if they really conversed together. If the brain of a bird has a speech-centre, it would be interesting to know whether it is larger in the tawny owl than in other birds.

They never normally hoot so close to the house, and I hope they will not come often to startle me at my window, but at least the owl must have been as alarmed as I was, for I reached up and pushed it into space, tipping it off by its stiff tail-feathers.

All the birds are closer to us now the Winter is here, and this morning Peter found a dead robin on the windowsill in the spare bedroom. There it lay with its legs in the air like the picture of Cock Robin in the nursery rhymes. I suppose it came into the house as they all do, and somehow got shut in the bedroom. But it must have been a stranger, for even with the door shut there is a broken windowpane which the regulars know all about, making straight for it as I chase them out.

It looked so pathetically frail and slight that I weighed it. Not quite half an ounce. Nine robins to the quarter-pound, like chocolates. And now of course it is asleep in the yellow cot in the dolls'-house. But as a doll it is much less obliging than mice. Its legs are too spikey and its tail will not fit in. They might cut off the end feathers, John suggested, but Peter, after deep thought, decided not. He didn't think the robin would like it, it would make it look silly.

It is always pathetic how creatures dead or ill or in trouble seem smaller than usual. Humans too. As if happiness and prosperity took up more room than misery. And people back from vigorous holidays are always quite alarmingly expanded, bringing with them an aura of wider horizons and higher skies than we stay-at-homes have known. They talk to you, even in the house, as if they were on a hill-top, and the restricted garden feels like the deck of a ship. They wear their clothes with a more assured air, and all one's own preoccupations seem very small and stale.

But it fades as quickly as the sun-tan, this larger-than-lifeness. Quite soon they can be brought into the house, even the door of a room can be closed behind them, without feeling they are being shut in a box.

WE met an old woman in the lane today who talked about the pebbles of her eyes, and ever since I have said to myself: "The fins of her eyelids look most teeming blue," and wondered all day what Webster meant by such magical mermaidy nonsense. But perhaps it is only that fins should be veins—the Elizabethan belief that pregnant women had blue-veined eyelids. She was, after all, the poor Duchess of Malfi, going to bring forth her son the very same evening. Or was it absurdly *twin* sons? Though perhaps that was someone else equally incongruous to us in high romantic tragedy. But the Elizabethans would not have minded. They kept their sense of humour for the bits which were meant to be funny, and did not let it leak out where it was not wanted, as we do. For I always want to laugh at the piles of corpses at the end of *Hamlet*, and it must have been even more ridiculous when they all had to get up and walk off again without a curtain. But nothing matters, for the poetry carries all the absurdities like a great wind.

The Duchess has always been one of my favourite heroines, for she dies in such fine style. No heroics, no appeals for pity, no wild lamenting of her fate (though

really she well might), but only a bitter, brave irony in
the face of death:

BOSOLA: *Doth not death fright you?*
DUCHESS: *Who would be afraid on't,*
          knowing to meet such excellent company
          in the other world?
BOSOLA: *Yet, methinks,*
          The manner of your death should much
              afflict you:
          This cord should terrify you.
DUCHESS: *Not a whit:*
          What would it pleasure me to have my
              throat cut
          with diamonds? or to be smothered
              with cassia? or to be shot to death with
                  pearls?

That, after all, is how duchesses should die, not like
lesser mortals, and the Elizabethans seem fantastic creatures always, strange and brilliant against a darkly sinister background. It is hard to believe that in a few generations these vivid, obsessed, unpredictable, haunted
figures would become the eighteenth century. It is a sea-
change as complete as the birth of the mild and conscientious modern Danes from the Vikings who were the
scourge of the north.

THE local big house has had a sale, and I went to look
round with the dealers, delighted at the chance to go over
the eighteenth-century mansion. But although I come to
appreciate them at last, the eighteenth-century interiors
have seemed till now to be at the same time both too
restrained and too fussy. They have lacked poetry. To

the young, the best English furniture, like so many best things English, is in too devastatingly good taste. Adam and Chippendale, Hepplewhite and Sheraton, they are irreproachable. Only Regency furniture has sometimes a half-fantastic vitality as un-English as the Elizabethans.

If English furniture is almost too well behaved, so too are English clothes. Every dress-designer must have at the back of his mind some ideal woman for whom his clothes are intended, and for the English she is a lady. Attractive, of course, but still, above all else, a lady, that particular English invention. The French ideal, so one must suppose from the clothes, is a very superior courtesan, and the American—well, I have never been to America, but I think some sort of young girl on a campus, whatever that may be.

This explains a great deal: why the Americans make good playclothes; why French clothes are sought all the world over; why English clothes are valued more for their quality than their appeal. For a brilliant courtesan is a cosmopolitan, but the English lady a very local and acquired taste. It explains too why American adults often dress so unsuitably, and why the gap between *haute couture* and French domestic fashions is so abysmal. In England, where everyone can at least aim at looking like a lady, as distinct from the more unlikely ideal of a teenager or Mme de Pompadour, in England clothes vary more in quality than in style, from duchess to shopgirl. And since being a lady is an almost sexless occupation, it can equally include being a gentleman and so produce in England the best men's clothes in the world.

TODAY the hunt met in the village, and we all went to watch. John climbed to the top of a fence for a better view, and chanted steadily to himself: "Hungry as a hunter. Hungry as a hunter. Hunters are very hungry. Hunters eat sandwiches" (pronounced with great care). "And horses eat sandwiches. Only sometimes they eat hay. Foxes don't eat sandwiches. Foxes eat chickens. Foxes are very, *very* naughty. Bang, bang. Tomorrow we shot a fox." (Luckily no one else was listening.) "Bang, bang. Fall down dead."

Then on again after a pause. "Hunters have funny hats. Hunters have funny horses. Too thin. Not farm horses. Farm horses have furry legs."

At the moment he has an engaging way of bringing me bits of information as if they were presents. He rushes up, tips his head so far back that his mouth will not stay shut, and out it comes. "The pig's got out," or: "We found an egg in the haystack," or: "Poor Peter's wet *right* through." Very frank and very serious. For children are always serious except on the occasions which they themselves recognize as games. It is stupid of us to think that their playing is frivolous, infuriating for them to be teased constantly.

"Yes," said Peter, listening before he went to bed to someone singing on the wireless. "Yes, I'm a bit of a good singer too. Only I don't sing at nights. I sing at mornings. Then it's beautiful. It sounds like crying." No faintest ghost of a smile. And I have heard it; it does sound like crying.

Peter's idea of good singers may sound like crying, but I have another way to tell, and just as easy. The real and rare ones simply open their mouths, and the singing comes out. An effortless flow like a river. They do nothing about it at all. No straining for high notes, no pushing out the volume, no jerky phrases, no wobbling, no filling up with breath for the long runs, no effort at all, except now and then to close their mouths and stop the lovely noise which happens of itself as soon as they open their mouths to let it come out.

If the first note sounds like that, there is no need to know any more, but simply sit back happy and let them sing whatever they will, even Dido's farewell to Æneas from Purcell's opera, which is the loveliest song in the world, and needs the loveliest voice.

But singers as good as that are as rare as the green-feathered Phœnix. For any good performer must have not only a good instrument, but the inborn gift to play on it. And though we can bring the fine violin for the fine player, we can scarcely transplant someone's good voice to the throat of someone else who has the skill to sing with it. It seems a pity, but we can only sit and hope that voice and skill may sometimes coincide.

The wireless went off in the middle of the concert. Half an hour's silence before it came tentatively hiccuping back to normal. And at the end an apologetic voice. They were sorry, it said. It was a technical breakdown. It was a fault in the transmitter. He apologized.

How charming of him to come and tell us. And how odd. Did he suppose we thought he had switched it off for fun? Or that the orchestra had suddenly disappeared through the floor? But no odder than little boys who ask always: "Please can you tell me the right time?" Never simply the time, but always the *right* time, as if we might otherwise invent some quite unlikely hour to tease them.

BERTRAND RUSSELL has become a curiously moving radio figure, old and very fine. That dry, quiet voice which sounds so unhurried, yet covers the intellectual ground at such breathless speed for us struggling after. Patient and gentle as the strong are gentle, so that one cannot help thinking how much more apt as a motto "Out of the strong cometh forth sweetness" would be for him than for Mr. Lyle on the treacle tin. "Lion's Golden Syrup" the children call it, equating the name with the picture.

And he is tired, as if his enthusiasms, like other men's passions, had burnt themselves out, withered in the clear light of his intellect, leaving only pity and a sardonic wit. One sees his mind as a light growing steadily in height and brilliance until his whole landscape is illuminated with truth, bright and without mysteries. For if truth is a clear light over wide landscapes, it is not all gain. We long, in too great clarity, for Proust's shifting passions and Traherne's "shadowy exaltations." In the end the clear outlines seem hard and unsympathetic like a room lit with an unshaded lamp.

Too great clarity. For our faults are the exaggeration of our virtues, the aspects of our good qualities which irritate other people. To us ourselves they are meaningless and unconscious. The good are prigs, the high-spirited hearty, the pitiful sentimental. If we are conscious of our faults at all, it is only as an unimportant mistake of emphasis, and not as evils.

Evil is not that. Evil for each man is different and personal. We can only judge it in ourselves, since it is what each of us feels to be the negation of our own good. For the generous it is meanness; for the prudent, waste; for the chaste, prostitution; for the loving, coldness. For Bertrand Russell, bigotry, prejudice, and intellectual darkness.

And because we feel that his whole mind is clear and lucid, that he has arrived now at his own state of grace, he leaves so moving an impression of goodness. Like the family of intellectually brilliant brothers in Giraudoux's novel *Bella,* "*il traite la vie par la lumière comme un cancer.*"

We are all adrift on a lonely, indifferent sea, carried ignorantly through our lives from one dark horizon to the other. Most of us are in sheltering boats against the bottomless ocean, shut in with religions, with causes we believe in, communities we belong to, family groups. These make the intellectual boundaries of our world, we see no further, only sometimes drawn, despite ourselves, to look over the side and be left for days after appalled at the hopeless enormity of the view.

We can live happily in our narrow boat and never know the sea is there until it drowns us at last. And even death, for most of us, comes unawares. "*Peu de gens connaissent la mort.*" It is Rochefoucauld speaking. "*On ne la souffre pas ordinairement par résolution, mais par stupidité et par coutume.*"

But there are some who die daily, the unhappy ones who face life without the merciful delusions, who swim defenceless in the icy sea. Swift is there, and Shakespeare, who wrote *Hamlet,* and Botticelli, though for him the waves are gentle, and Hopkins, since his religion failed him, and Henry James, though he swims like an angel and is discreet. And Mozart. But Mozart is of his time's culture, though conscious always of the desolate horizon in his sad, lovely music.

For Mozart does seem deeply sad beneath his urbanity. Not self-consciously, like those who say: "Look. Others are happy, but I am wretched," seeing a world of gladness from which they are only barred by some accident. For Mozart there *is* no joyous world. "Here," he says, "is laughing and singing and dancing, and see, at heart it is sad." His gayest songs are his most mournful, like Prior, who said: *"Je suis triste quand je crie 'Banissons la mélancholie.'"*

All the scientists are swimmers in the great sea, the astronomers and physicists and mathematicians, and Bertrand Russell. But they are born sea-creatures, untroubled by warm blood and human lungs. For them the old sheltering beliefs are restrictions only, and they break free impatiently to Bertrand Russell's intellectual freedom. If they are conscious of the sea more than a fish is, they feel it eagerly as limitless opportunity, and only Pascal was dismayed.

The travellers in boats work hopefully, believing they steer their ship; yet it only drifts on the deep prevailing currents, and their most earnest efforts make scarcely a ripple. Still, if one is a humanitarian and lucky enough to be born in a current of social reform, it is easy to believe that you yourself are moving the ship, as the great Victorian reformers believed to their salvation. It is not, after all, what we *do* which matters to our soul's health, but what we believe that we are doing, like John taming his beetles. And Communists now must surely feel that it is their efforts which are changing the world, even though we are all carried, whichever way we may try to steer, on the irresistible stream of the evolution of states into ant-like communities.

For waiting in the chattering queue at the Food Office, no one could help being conscious that a new race of man is evolving to fit the new world he must live in. Industrial man is replacing agricultural man. It is not only that more people live in towns or work in factories, but that people are changing in kind. The cowman now feels closer to his electric milking-machine than to his cows, and for every labourer who can thatch a hayrick there are a dozen who can take a tractor to pieces. Even since

we came to live here, the actual countryside is more deserted, even though the local town has doubled its inhabitants. There are fewer figures blackberrying along
the hedges or wandering the fields for mushrooms, many
more at the bus-stops waiting to be carried to the town
with its cinemas and shops.

The new race will be different, but neither better nor
worse, whatever the diehards may say. Worse, they say,
of course, but no animal can be expected to see the virtues
of the new one which supplants it. Besides, when cultures
change, the old virtues are lost faster than the new ones
develop. There is a period of semi-barbarism before the
new pattern emerges. So the old initiative and self-re-
liance and natural good taste (so my elders tell me of a
world I never knew) are already falling away, while we
can still only dimly guess at what will be the virtues of
the new society which is coming. Co-operation perhaps,
and a feeling of world-wide sympathy with one's fellow
creatures which ignores the old patriotism as parochial
prejudice. But it is too soon to tell.

Even the physical type is changing, so the records tell
us. Tall people with blue eyes and fair hair are growing
rarer everywhere, even in Scandinavia, being a type un-
suited, it seems, to life in cities. The new industrial population is smaller and quicker, with hazel eyes and brownish hair. I look round our blue-eyed tea-table and think
that none of us is meant for the new world, which seems
a pity.

The new race which inherits the world will have new
values which we cannot even guess at yet; and a new
culture which must surely come from science, as the
classical culture comes from the humanities, and older
ones from religion. Poetry, painting, and music may have
no place in the new world, and looking back, Einstein

may seem the greatest artist of our age, with his disquieting and beautiful vision of the universe. Though I, being of the old world and no mathematician at all, can only catch it in fitful glimpses. Science now, and not the humanities, is the new land for the imagination, for the artist's sense of wonder and beauty, and any philosophy of the future must somehow include the receding nebulæ and the structure of the atom.

How thankful I am that I shall not have to struggle with it, and how thankful too that although the change may be happening at breakneck speed by evolutionary standards, for us human ephemera it is no more than a gradual shifting of emphasis. There will be enough of the old world left for me to live my life out with my old-fashioned ideas, and my great-great-grandchildren will no more want to live in my world than I want to live in Ancient Egypt.

And in the end, perhaps there will not be so great a difference. The new aristocracy will gradually emerge— of bureaucrats or scientists, one supposes—and in a thousand years or so it may well be indistinguishable from any other aristocracy. For the highly privileged of every culture seem to be as limited in their pleasures as anyone else. Building, patronizing the arts, living luxuriously— there seems never to have been much else, whatever their resources, and there seems no reason why the aristocrats of the future should be any different.

In another thousand years there may even be another classical revival, and it would be amusing to know whether it will be direct from the Greeks or secondhand through our own Renaissance.

A KIND friend, well-meaning, but with no children of her own to help, has sent John and Peter a book of stories without pictures, and they are reasonably puzzled. "Look," they say, "it hasn't got any pictures. It's the sort *you* read. Look. No pictures at all. It must be for you."

I remember very well, long after I could read, how I hated books without pictures. It was not that one needed the pictures for illustration, for one's own imagined story was much too vivid for anyone else's drawings to make much difference. But the book itself was dull. For books, to a child, are another kind of toy, and they must be amusing simply as objects in themselves. So a book without pictures is as sullen as a street of all houses and no shops, as uninteresting as a room without toys, as uninviting as a letter to a child on paper simply when it could have been written on a picture post-card.

But she sent too, perhaps to make up for the pictures, a whole bundle of picture post-cards, coloured photographs of the Grand Tour, for the children to cut up and make scraps, she said. But they have not made scraps, they have made windmills. All morning they have bothered me to stop baking apple pies and treacle tarts and to make them windmills instead.

First the card must be cut square, then diagonally inwards from the corners, then the points curved over, and all mounted on a stick with a pin. And as each one is finished, the children run off and plant them like sudden stiff flowers to spin in rows on the lawn. The improbable blue of a Mediterranean sky blurring in the soft, rainy wind, Mount Vesuvius spinning under the willows.

From time to time they seize one in each hand and rush down the orchard path into the gale of the west wind, wildly excited. I think they half hope to take off like aeroplanes behind their propellers, to soar over the tree-tops as one does in dreams.

AUTUMN

And because the kitchen windows have been blurred with the gusty rain, it is as if all day I have watched them through tears, pathetic small figures under the great tossing trees.

FOR three days now we have been shut in by thick fog, and we all grow tired of so cramped a life.

At first it has a charm of its own, this clean country mist drifting thick or thin like clouds on a mountain. It gives the curiously intimate feel of being in a tent, but a moving tent, with ourselves as the tentpole and the walls equidistant wherever we go. If we move our enclosure so that it takes in some tree-stump overgrown with ivy, some hedge-bottom glistening with wet, the hedge and the ivy at once become as close and vivid as if we had taken them indoors, which is surely one of the reasons for picking flowers, that they show as more intensely themselves against the different indoor background.

There are days at the seaside when the sea mist rolls inland and swallows us. We feel we are no longer on the solid edge of the land, but floated off into the different world of the sea. And so it is here. Dragons live at the end of the orchard, the children pretend, and half believe it, for anything can happen beyond the wall of the fog.

But it has gone on too long now. One day is amusing, but this is the third time we have wakened to our limited world. Another day and I shall believe with Bishop Berkeley, against my own humbler convictions, that the world only exists as we perceive it. From seeing so long nothing but the nearer apple tres, I begin to doubt that anything does exist beyond, except in my imagination. If I walk to the far field gate, I create, as I approach, the flinty drive and the bordering hedge. But they disappear behind me as I pass, and perhaps no longer exist except in my memory. I suppose it is only another step to believing that the fields and hills of fine days are equally insubstantial, a view I have imagined for my own pleasure.

But how quite astonishingly conceited. I know perfectly well that I could never by any chance imagine anything even remotely as satisfactory as the view from the gate, nor anything as exquisitely ingenious as the humblest plant. And how does he explain that we all see much the same world around us? There are differences, of course, since we are all differently imperfect instruments for recording outside reality, but we all see the sun as round and bright at midday, and if we kick a stone to prove our point, like Doctor Johnson, we all hurt our toes.

For Bishop Berkeley is as egocentric as the old astronomers, who believed the earth was the centre of the universe, and the sky of stars only an embroidered tent for the night. The tree which goes on growing on the desert island he explains by his own religious casuistry, but what of all the past ages before man existed? What of the worlds of fossils? But perhaps they did not dig them up enough in those days to worry him.

The universe, he says, is a dream in the mind of God. If he really believes that man can imagine a god capable of dreaming such magnificent wonder, then there really can be no answer.

But the fog goes on and on, and we are tired of being shut in. If I had an aeroplane, I would fly us straight up into the open sunshine above, since with all respect to the Bishop, we none of us seem able to perceive it for ourselves down here.

How strange it would be to live in a land of constant fog, so that we knew it was hilly only because we had to change gear in our motor-cars, and was big only because it took a long time to travel from one place to another by compass.

But I grow childish from living too close to the children. I shall read Gilbert White and walk round Selbourne in his civilizing company.

The telephone rang in the night, and hurrying downstairs to answer it before it should wake the children too, there was still time for the wild, improbable hope that it might be my husband suddenly back in England.

But time too, as I woke up on the way down, to realize that I would not really like him back suddenly out of the night; that I wanted a properly heralded homecoming. Not only because looking forward to a promised pleasure is in itself the most satisfactory of pleasures, but because the big things should have a certain setting and dignity, and not just pop up like a jack-in-a-box.

"That's a government," said John, showing me a pile of toys. "A government's when a lot of cars and lorries bump into each other. And a cornucopia" (pronounced slowly and carefully as if it were five separate words), "a cor-nu-co-pi-a's an old cow's horn with apples in it."

He is fascinated always by words, and soon I will tell him some of my favourites. Popocatepetl, like a magic charm, and Azochloramid, a lazy golden word, and Tillaquils, like flowers. Except for the volcano, I have no idea where I found them or what they mean, but all the best words are what the *Oxford English Dictionary* calls "of obscure origin," like Cock-a-hoop.

But John has his own words. Celery, Paralena, Sickerty, Hayborn, Wallup. Who could guess they were names of engines? He walks round the house chanting to himself:

AUTUMN

"Celery, Sickerty, Hayborn, and Wallup,
Celery, Sickerty, Hayborn, and Wallup,"

over and over. And of these Hayborn is ever and always the favourite, a wheel-less, funnel-less, tender-less block, with only here and there a trace of paint to show that it began as a brave red wooden engine.

"Lion and lioness," he shouted at the top of his voice, over and over.

"What about them?" I shouted back.

"The lion's the father and the lioness is the mother. What's a lion's nanny called?"

They didn't have one, I said.

"Well, what's a kangaroo's nanny called?"

I said they didn't have one either, and asked him what a hedgehog's nanny's called.

"Yes," he said, delighted that I would play, "and what's an ear-wig's nanny called? And what's a tea-wig's nanny called? And what's a dinny-danny called?" getting more and more James Joyce.

I shall miss it when they are too old to be danced off into nonsense, like playing Handy-Pandy, which always ends in hilarious uproar however slowly and soberly one starts. (I still wonder, and have never found out, what is French Almond Rock?)

I shall miss having teddy bears as the main business of our packing, finding engines behind every cushion, and pictures chalked all over the paths. I shall miss the doll's-house peopled with sleeping mice, and the sand-pit with its helter-skelters for marbles to run down, and the constant hedge of dungarees and Wellington boots drying round the kitchen fire.

I shall miss all our life here when we have left it, and the Farmer who has been, through these uneasy years,

. 238 .

our surest friend. He lives in the harsh new house, the desirable modern residence with wash-basins in every bedroom, which they built when they left this house to dream in the orchard. He is our closest friend and only neighbour, and one of the few people I have ever known whom I trust completely. Not trust to be honest or brave, though that too, of course, but would trust in chaos.

For he is the exact antithesis of Eliot's Hollow Men. Old and failing, he is yet in complete control of his world, a logical, relevant world, real even in enveloping nightmare. Whatever happened, Kafka's agonizing anxieties would never beset him. Disaster would be real, with definite things to be done about it. His world would still be sane.

He tells us endless stories of how he used to thresh by hand—"thrash" he calls it; of how he would help as a boy at the local great house when Edward VII came down for gay week-ends, of how he outwitted a rival farmer with true peasant cunning. It is forty years ago now, but he still remembers what wheat he grew in what field as vividly as if he saw it springing green at his feet.

He tells us how to know a sheep's age by its increasing number of teeth; the points to look for in a good milch cow; which variety of grain best suits which soil. And in return I tell him the names of birds and flowers which he has seen every day of his life and being a true countryman, which I am not, knows no name for.

But soon he will die, and my world will seem less safe simply to know that his no longer exists. People who are going to die have an indefinable look of being somehow fragile inside. They may not be ill, or even weak. The Farmer is big and brown, and works a full day with the hay-makers, but already he has this air of something vital going to pieces inside, and I think any morning they will come to tell me they have found him dead.

THERE is a stage with people we love when we are no longer separate from them, but so close in sympathy that we live through them as directly as through ourselves. Seeing them, suddenly we feel, not that we are looking at another person, but at our own self, more intimate and personal than any reflection in the mirror. "Why, there I am," we think, seeing them walk towards us down the path. "That's what I look like," and we push back our hair because theirs is in their eyes.

Long before this we have shared their reactions and emotions. The noise we know they dislike becomes for us too, even when they are not there, an exquisite irritation. Because they dislike dogs, we too find them tiresome. We can read Proust at last because he is their favourite writer.

But now we share their very senses. We are cold with them, warm with them, tired with them, restless with them. We smell as acutely as they the rose they have buried their nose in. When they drink, it is we who savour the coffee, even so actually that a moment after we apologize for taking their cup which we had never touched. We no longer know whether they have sneezed or we have, nor which of us is thirsty from walking in the heat. Bewilderingly we are no longer separate.

So it must always have been between people, but now, absurdly, I have become part of this house which I love. "There," I feel with relief, coming back to it among the orchard trees. "Yes. There I am." I never thought to mistake myself for bricks and mortar, but so it is. There is one view especially where looking at the house is like looking into the inside of my own head.

Even our physical lives are no longer independent. I
dread the nights of storm when the wind roars like a bull
in the wide chimneys, and the fragile old tiles slide rattling down the roof, and the whole house creaks and
sways in its oak frame. I sigh with pleasure in the first
hot sun of the year, feeling the porous bricks dry out
after the Winter damp. And in the cold and frost I live
in such a mystic sympathy with the rambling, ridiculous
plumbing, that if a pipe burst in the night I think I should
wake up in trouble.

We envy people we love for being always in their own
loved company, for we must leave them and somehow
occupy ourselves through the pointless time until we are
together again. So I envy this house which need never
leave the atmosphere it creates so strongly. For we shall
leave it, and though the children will not remember, I
know that, half unconsciously, I shall be homesick for it
all the rest of my life.

There are some love-affairs which from the beginning
have the poignancy of all things which cannot last, and
this house is like that. For the children must go to school,
and my husband must work in London. And when we
have gone away I shall remember it in many different
moods, as one remembers the people one loves. In the
Winter dusk, or mellow in mellow Autumn weather, but
most piercingly of all on warm Spring evenings in a
greenish twilight in a froth of fool's parsley.

And when we go, it will be left deserted again, with
the orchard weeds closing in like a green engulfing sea,
and the sunlight moving round the empty rooms. And
on the nursery wall, hidden behind the curtain so that
they should not be covered up in the yearly distempering,
the children's heights will still be marked on ascending
dated lines—John, September 11th, and Peter an inch

above him. But the children will be gone, lost as completely as if they were dead. Changed into different people, into schoolboys and strange young men, not even remembering the house which sheltered them through the war.

It is sad, as one grows less young and less ruthless, to break off any relationship for good. A loss, like a root chopped off, a narrowing of the sources of living.

For after a certain time—the end of youth perhaps, which does not die all at once, but after painful rallyings and relapses—one will not be able to grow new roots. The relationships of middle-age will be only urbane surface meetings, pleasant like Autumn sunshine, but one will make nothing of them, wan and sapless. For to be moved is to be still young, and perhaps after youth we should make no final decisions.

THE first snow of the Winter is falling, in delicate star-shaped crystals whose minute patterns we can just see. And I wonder where, in the gamut of size in the universe, human vision lies. It must be a very narrow range, in a scale where the distances of stars are measured in light-years and the invisible atom is a complicated structure. Yet we see nothing much bigger than the view from our picnic hill, nor smaller than the figures of its contours on the map. And though our sight does well enough for practical living, we lose a great deal. The patterns of snow-flakes we can just see, but not the creatures in a drop of pond-water, nor the designs of cells, nor the arrangement of crystals.

Perhaps we lose as much at the large end, for one can imagine great patterns of land and sea, the changing shapes of continents as the earth spins away, and lovely light round the edge of the world. We might well invent a god simply to feel that such fine scenic effects were not wasted. And after all it would be a more disinterested reason than the usual one, that we cannot face our cosmic loneliness and insignificance.

Yet we *must* face them, or delude ourselves. If man's greatness is his mind, then he must see clearly and bravely, and refuse all comforting delusions. Human life, says Sartre, begins on the far side of despair.

But it is not easy to live with the knowledge that we are in an alien and indifferent universe, for the utter indifference of the stars is far more terrible than enmity. Beside it our savagest wars seem warm and friendly encounters.

It is hard to accept that we are here for no purpose which we can even vaguely understand. That our separate lives concern no one at all but ourselves. That we shall disappear like all the other races of animals which have dominated the earth, and our only trace will be beds of fossils in the quaternary rocks.

We must accept that goodness, pity, mercy, justice, all the values we live by, do not exist outside our own minds. That they are an invention of the human animal in its present stage of evolution. That they have no validity beyond our own reactions, and we must value them, not because they correspond to any ultimate standards, but because man is only happy as a virtuous creature.

We must accept that of our human values, beauty is the only one which seems to exist outside ourselves. That even this last intellectual coherence may well be a delusion. That we must manage as best we can.

This book was set on the Linotype in Janson, a recutting made direct from the type cast from matrices (now in possession of the Stempel foundry, Frankfurt am Main) made by Anton Janson some time between 1660 and 1687. This type is an excellent example of the influential and singularly sturdy Dutch types that prevailed in England prior to Caslon. It was from the Dutch types that Caslon developed his own designs.

Of Janson's origin nothing is known. He may have been a relative of Justus Janson, a printer of Danish birth who practised in Leipzig from 1614 to 1635. Some time between 1657 and 1668 Anton Janson, a punch-cutter and type-founder, bought from the Leipzig printer Johann Erich Hahn the type-foundry which had formerly been a part of the printing house of M. Friedrich Lankisch. Janson's types were first shown in a specimen sheet issued at Leipzig about 1675. Janson's successor, and perhaps his son-in-law, Johann Karl Edling, issued a specimen sheet of Janson types in 1689.

The book was composed, printed, and bound by KINGSPORT PRESS, INC., *Kingsport, Tennessee.* Designed *by* HARRY FORD.